MOBY-DICK

Herman Melville

EDITORIAL DIRECTOR Laurie Barnett
DIRECTOR OF TECHNOLOGY Tammy Hepps

SERIES EDITOR John Crowther
MANAGING EDITOR Vincent Janoski

WRITERS Jia-Rui Chong, Melissa Martin, Jim Cocola
EDITORS John Crowther, Boomie Aglietti, John Crowther, Justin Kestler

This edition published by Spark Publishing

Spark Publishing
A Division of SparkNotes LLC
120 Fifth Avenue, 8th Floor
New York, NY 10011

Any book purchased without a cover is stolen property, reported as "unsold and
destroyed" to the Publisher, who receives no payment for such "stripped books."

Please submit all comments and questions or report errors to www.sparknotes.com/errors

Printed and bound in the United States

ISBN 1-58663-415-1

Introduction:
Stopping to Buy SparkNotes on a Snowy Evening

Whose words these are you *think* you know.
Your paper's due tomorrow, though;
We're glad to see you stopping here
To get some help before you go.

Lost your course? You'll find it here.
Face tests and essays without fear.
Between the words, good grades at stake:
Get great results throughout the year.

Once school bells caused your heart to quake
As teachers circled each mistake.
Use SparkNotes and no longer weep,
Ace every single test you take.

Yes, books are lovely, dark, and deep,
But only what you grasp you keep,
With hours to go before you sleep,
With hours to go before you sleep.

Contents

CONTEXT   1

PLOT OVERVIEW   3

CHARACTER LIST   6

ANALYSIS OF MAJOR CHARACTERS   10
  ISHMAEL   10
  AHAB   10
  MOBY DICK   11
  STARBUCK, STUBB, AND FLASK   11

THEMES, MOTIFS & SYMBOLS   13
  THE LIMITS OF KNOWLEDGE   13
  THE DECEPTIVENESS OF FATE   13
  THE EXPLOITATIVE NATURE OF WHALING   14
  WHITENESS   14
  SURFACES AND DEPTHS   15
  THE PEQUOD   15
  MOBY DICK   15
  QUEEQUEG'S COFFIN   16

SUMMARY & ANALYSIS   17
  ETYMOLOGY & EXTRACTS   17
  CHAPTERS 1–9   18
  CHAPTERS 10–21   22
  CHAPTERS 22–31   27
  CHAPTERS 32–40   30
  CHAPTERS 41–47   34
  CHAPTERS 48–54   37
  CHAPTERS 55–65   41
  CHAPTERS 66–73   44
  CHAPTERS 74–81   48
  CHAPTERS 82–92   51
  CHAPTERS 93–101   55
  CHAPTERS 102–114   59
  CHAPTERS 115–125   63

CHAPTERS 126–132   67
CHAPTER 133–EPILOGUE   69

IMPORTANT QUOTATIONS EXPLAINED   73

KEY FACTS   78

STUDY QUESTIONS & ESSAY TOPICS   81
  STUDY QUESTIONS   81
  SUGGESTED ESSAY TOPICS   83

REVIEW & RESOURCES   84
  QUIZ   84
  SUGGESTIONS FOR FURTHER READING   89

CONTEXT

HERMAN MELVILLE WAS BORN in New York City in 1819, the third of eight children born to Maria Gansevoort Melville and Allan Melville, a prosperous importer of foreign goods. When the family business failed at the end of the 1820s, the Melvilles relocated to Albany in an attempt to revive their fortunes. A string of further bad luck and overwork, however, drove his father to an early grave, and the young Melville was forced to start working in a bank at the age of thirteen.

After a few more years of formal education, Melville left school at eighteen to become an elementary school teacher. This career was abruptly cut short and followed by a brief tenure as a newspaper reporter. Running out of alternatives on land, Melville made his first sea voyage at nineteen, as a merchant sailor on a ship bound for Liverpool, England. He returned to America the next summer to seek his fortune in the West. After settling briefly in Illinois, he went back east in the face of continuing financial difficulties.

Finally, driven to desperation at twenty-one, Melville committed to a whaling voyage of indefinite destination and scale on board a ship called the *Acushnet*. This journey took him around the continent of South America, across the Pacific Ocean, and to the South Seas, where he abandoned ship with a fellow sailor in the summer of 1842, eighteen months after setting out from New York. The two men found themselves in the Marquesas Islands, where they accidentally wandered into the company of a tribe of cannibals. Lamed with a bad leg, Melville became separated from his companion and spent a month alone in the company of the natives. This experience later formed the core of his first novel, *Typee: A Peep at Polynesian Life,* published in 1846. An indeterminate mixture of fact and fiction, Melville's fanciful travel narrative remained the most popular and successful of his works during his lifetime.

Life among these natives and other exotic experiences abroad provided Melville with endless literary conceits. Armed with the voluminous knowledge obtained from constant reading while at sea, Melville wrote a series of novels detailing his adventures and his philosophy of life. *Typee* was followed by *Omoo* (1847) and *Mardi and a Voyage Thither* (1849), two more novels about his Polynesian experiences. *Redburn,* also published in 1849, is a fictionalized account of Melville's first voyage to Liverpool. His next novel, *White-Jacket; or The World in a Man-of-War,* published in 1850, is a generalized and allegorical account of life at sea aboard a warship. Through the lens of literary history, these first five novels are all seen as an apprenticeship to what is today considered Melville's masterpiece, *Moby-Dick; or The Whale,* which first appeared in 1851. A story of monomania aboard a whaling ship, *Moby-Dick* is a tremendously ambitious novel that functions at once as a documentary of life at sea and a vast philosophical allegory of life in general. No sacred subject is spared in this bleak and scathing critique of the known world, as Melville satirizes by turns religious traditions, moral values, and the literary and political figures of the day.

Melville was influenced in the writing of *Moby-Dick* by the work of Nathaniel Hawthorne, author of *The Scarlet Letter,* whom he met in 1850 and to whom he dedicated *Moby-Dick.* Melville had long admired Hawthorne's psychological depth and gothic grimness and associated Hawthorne with a new, distinctively American literature. Though the works of Shakespeare and Milton and stories in the Bible (especially the Old Testament) influenced *Moby-Dick,* Melville didn't look exclusively to celebrated cultural models. He drew on sources from popular culture as well; whaling narratives, for example, were popular in the nineteenth century. Melville relied on Thomas Beale's encyclopedic *Natural History of the Sperm Whale* and the narrative *Etchings of a Whaling Cruise,* by J. Ross Browne.

By the 1850s, whaling was a dying industry. Whales had been hunted into near extinction, and substitutes for whale oil had been found. Despite its range of cultural references and affiliation with popular genres, *Moby-Dick* was a failure. Its reception led Melville to defy his critics by writing in an increasingly experimental style and eventually forsaking novels in favor of poetry. He died in 1891.

Moby-Dick remained largely ignored until the 1920s, when it was rediscovered and promoted by literary historians interested in constructing an American literary tradition. To these critics, *Moby-Dick* was both a seminal work elaborating on classic American themes, such as religion, fate, and economic expansion, and a radically experimental anachronism that anticipated Modernism in its outsized scope and pastiche of forms. It stands alongside James Joyce's *Ulysses* and Laurence Sterne's *Tristram Shandy* as a novel that appears bizarre to the point of being unreadable but proves to be infinitely open to interpretation and discovery.

PLOT OVERVIEW

ISHMAEL, THE NARRATOR, ANNOUNCES his intent to ship aboard a whaling vessel. He has made several voyages as a sailor but none as a whaler. He travels to New Bedford, Massachusetts, where he stays in a whalers' inn. Since the inn is rather full, he has to share a bed with a harpooner from the South Pacific named Queequeg. At first repulsed by Queequeg's strange habits and shocking appearance (Queequeg is covered with tattoos), Ishmael eventually comes to appreciate the man's generosity and kind spirit, and the two decide to seek work on a whaling vessel together. They take a ferry to Nantucket, the traditional capital of the whaling industry. There they secure berths on the *Pequod*, a savage-looking ship adorned with the bones and teeth of sperm whales. Peleg and Bildad, the *Pequod*'s Quaker owners, drive a hard bargain in terms of salary. They also mention the ship's mysterious captain, Ahab, who is still recovering from losing his leg in an encounter with a sperm whale on his last voyage.

The *Pequod* leaves Nantucket on a cold Christmas Day with a crew made up of men from many different countries and races. Soon the ship is in warmer waters, and Ahab makes his first appearance on deck, balancing gingerly on his false leg, which is made from a sperm whale's jaw. He announces his desire to pursue and kill Moby Dick, the legendary great white whale who took his leg, because he sees this whale as the embodiment of evil. Ahab nails a gold doubloon to the mast and declares that it will be the prize for the first man to sight the whale. As the *Pequod* sails toward the southern tip of Africa, whales are sighted and unsuccessfully hunted. During the hunt, a group of men, none of whom anyone on the ship's crew has seen before on the voyage, emerges from the hold. The men's leader is an exotic-looking man named Fedallah. These men constitute Ahab's private harpoon crew, smuggled aboard in defiance of Bildad and Peleg. Ahab hopes that their skills and Fedallah's prophetic abilities will help him in his hunt for Moby Dick.

The *Pequod* rounds Africa and enters the Indian Ocean. A few whales are successfully caught and processed for their oil. From time to time, the ship encounters other whaling vessels. Ahab always demands information about Moby Dick from their captains. One of the ships, the *Jeroboam*, carries Gabriel, a crazed prophet who predicts doom for anyone who threatens Moby Dick. His predictions seem to carry some weight, as those aboard his ship who have hunted the whale have met disaster. While trying to drain the oil from the head of a captured sperm whale, Tashtego, one of the *Pequod*'s harpooners, falls into the whale's voluminous head, which then rips free of the ship and begins to sink. Queequeg saves Tashtego by diving into the ocean and cutting into the slowly sinking head.

During another whale hunt, Pip, the *Pequod*'s black cabin boy, jumps from a whaleboat and is left behind in the middle of the ocean. He goes insane as the result of the experience and becomes a crazy but prophetic jester for the ship. Soon after, the *Pequod* meets the *Samuel Enderby,* a whaling ship whose skipper, Captain Boomer, has lost an arm in an encounter with Moby Dick. The two captains discuss the whale; Boomer, happy simply to have survived his encounter, cannot understand Ahab's lust for vengeance. Not long after, Queequeg falls ill and has the ship's carpenter make him a coffin in anticipation of his death. He recovers, however, and the coffin eventually becomes the *Pequod*'s replacement life buoy.

Ahab orders a harpoon forged in the expectation that he will soon encounter Moby Dick. He baptizes the harpoon with the blood of the *Pequod*'s three harpooners. The *Pequod* kills several more whales. Issuing a prophecy about Ahab's death, Fedallah declares that Ahab will first see two hearses, the second of which will be made only from American wood, and that he will be killed by hemp rope. Ahab interprets these words to mean that he will not die at sea, where there are no hearses and no hangings. A typhoon hits the *Pequod,* illuminating it with electrical fire. Ahab takes this occurrence as a sign of imminent confrontation and success, but Starbuck, the ship's first mate, takes it as a bad omen and considers killing Ahab to end the mad quest. After the storm ends, one of the sailors falls from the ship's masthead and drowns—a grim foreshadowing of what lies ahead.

Ahab's fervent desire to find and destroy Moby Dick continues to intensify, and the mad Pip is now his constant companion. The *Pequod* approaches the equator, where Ahab expects to find the great whale. The ship encounters two more whaling ships, the *Rachel* and the *Delight,* both of which have recently had fatal encounters with the whale. Ahab finally sights Moby Dick. The harpoon boats are launched, and Moby Dick attacks Ahab's harpoon boat, destroying it. The next day, Moby Dick is sighted again, and the boats are lowered once more. The whale is harpooned, but

Moby Dick again attacks Ahab's boat. Fedallah, trapped in the harpoon line, is dragged overboard to his death. Starbuck must maneuver the *Pequod* between Ahab and the angry whale.

On the third day, the boats are once again sent after Moby Dick, who once again attacks them. The men can see Fedallah's corpse lashed to the whale by the harpoon line. Moby Dick rams the *Pequod* and sinks it. Ahab is then caught in a harpoon line and hurled out of his harpoon boat to his death. All of the remaining whaleboats and men are caught in the vortex created by the sinking *Pequod* and pulled under to their deaths. Ishmael, who was thrown from a boat at the beginning of the chase, was far enough away to escape the whirlpool, and he alone survives. He floats atop Queequeg's coffin, which popped back up from the wreck, until he is picked up by the *Rachel,* which is still searching for the crewmen lost in her earlier encounter with Moby Dick.

CHARACTER LIST

Ishmael The narrator, and a junior member of the crew of the *Pequod*. Ishmael doesn't play a major role in the events of the novel, but much of the narrative is taken up by his eloquent, verbose, and extravagant discourse on whales and whaling.

Ahab The egomaniacal captain of the *Pequod*. Ahab lost his leg to Moby Dick. He is single-minded in his pursuit of the whale, using a mixture of charisma and terror to persuade his crew to join him. As a captain, he is dictatorial but not unfair. At moments he shows a compassionate side, caring for the insane Pip and musing on his wife and child back in Nantucket.

Moby Dick The great white sperm whale. Moby Dick, also referred to as the White Whale, is an infamous and dangerous threat to seamen, considered by Ahab the incarnation of evil and a fated nemesis.

Starbuck The first mate of the *Pequod*. Starbuck questions Ahab's judgment, first in private and later in public. He is a religious man who believes that Christianity offers a way to interpret the world around him, although he is not dogmatic or pushy about his beliefs. Starbuck acts as a conservative force against Ahab's mania.

Queequeg Starbuck's skilled harpooner and Ishmael's best friend. Queequeg was once a prince from a South Sea island who stowed away on a whaling ship in search of adventure. He is a composite of elements of African, Polynesian, Islamic, Christian, and Native American cultures. He is brave and generous, and enables Ishmael to see that race has no bearing on a man's character.

Stubb   The second mate of the *Pequod*. Stubb, chiefly characterized by his mischievous good humor, is easygoing and popular. He proves a bit of a nihilist, always trusting in fate and refusing to assign too much significance to anything.

Tashtego   Stubb's harpooner, Tashtego is a Gay Head Indian from Martha's Vineyard, one of the last of a tribe about to disappear. Tashtego performs many of the skilled tasks aboard the ship, such as tapping the case of spermaceti in the whale's head. Like Queequeg, Tashtego embodies certain characteristics of the "noble savage" and is meant to defy racial stereotypes. He is, however, more practical and less intellectual than Queequeg: like many a common sailor, Tashtego craves rum.

Flask   A native of Tisbury on Martha's Vineyard and the third mate of the *Pequod*. Short and stocky, Flask has a confrontational attitude and no reverence for anything. His stature has earned him the nickname "King-Post," because he resembles a certain type of short, square timber.

Daggoo   Flask's harpooner. Daggoo is a physically enormous, imperious- looking African. Like Queequeg, he stowed away on a whaling ship that stopped near his home. Daggoo is less prominent in the narrative than either Queequeg or Tashtego.

Pip   A young black boy who fills the role of a cabin boy or jester on the *Pequod*. Pip has a minimal role in the beginning of the narrative but becomes important when he goes insane after being left to drift alone in the sea for some time. Like the fools in Shakespeare's plays, he is half idiot and half prophet, often perceiving things that others don't.

CHARACTER LIST

Fedallah   A strange, "oriental" old Parsee (Persian fire-worshipper) whom Ahab has brought on board unbeknownst to most of the crew. Fedallah has a very striking appearance: around his head is a turban made from his own hair, and he wears a black Chinese jacket and pants. He is an almost supernaturally skilled hunter and also serves as a prophet to Ahab. Fedallah keeps his distance from the rest of the crew, who for their part view him with unease.

Peleg   A well-to-do retired whaleman of Nantucket and a Quaker. As one of the principal owners of the *Pequod,* Peleg, along with Captain Bildad, takes care of hiring the crew. When the two are negotiating wages for Ishmael and Queequeg, Peleg plays the generous one, although his salary offer is not terribly impressive.

Bildad   Another well-to-do Quaker ex-whaleman from Nantucket who owns a large share of the *Pequod.* Bildad is (or pretends to be) crustier than Peleg in negotiations over wages. Both men display a business sense and a bloodthirstiness unusual for Quakers, who are normally pacifists.

Father Mapple   A former whaleman and now the preacher in the New Bedford Whaleman's Chapel. Father Mapple delivers a sermon on Jonah and the whale in which he uses the Bible to address the whalemen's lives. Learned but also experienced, he is an example of someone whose trials have led him toward God rather than bitterness or revenge.

Captain Boomer   The jovial captain of the English whaling ship the *Samuel Enderby.* Boomer lost his arm in an accident involving Moby Dick. Unlike Ahab, Boomer is glad to have escaped with his life, and he sees further pursuit of the whale as madness. He is a foil for Ahab, as the two men react in different ways to a similar experience.

Gabriel   A sailor aboard the *Jeroboam*. Part of a Shaker sect, Gabriel has prophesied that Moby Dick is the incarnation of the Shaker god and that any attempts to harm him will result in disaster. His prophecies have been borne out by the death of the *Jeroboam*'s mate in a whale hunt and the plague that rages aboard the ship.

CHARACTER LIST

ANALYSIS OF MAJOR CHARACTERS

ISHMAEL

Despite his centrality to the story, Ishmael doesn't reveal much about himself to the reader. We know that he has gone to sea out of some deep spiritual malaise and that shipping aboard a whaler is his version of committing suicide—he believes that men aboard a whaling ship are lost to the world. It is apparent from Ishmael's frequent digressions on a wide range of subjects—from art, geology, and anatomy to legal codes and literature—that he is intelligent and well educated, yet he claims that a whaling ship has been "[his] Yale College and [his] Harvard." He seems to be a self-taught Renaissance man, good at everything but committed to nothing. Given the mythic, romantic aspects of *Moby-Dick*, it is perhaps fitting that its narrator should be an enigma: not everything in a story so dependent on fate and the seemingly supernatural needs to make perfect sense.

Additionally, Ishmael represents the fundamental contradiction between the story of *Moby-Dick* and its setting. Melville has created a profound and philosophically complicated tale and set it in a world of largely uneducated working-class men; Ishmael, thus, seems less a real character than an instrument of the author. No one else aboard the *Pequod* possesses the proper combination of intellect and experience to tell this story. Indeed, at times even Ishmael fails Melville's purposes, and he disappears from the story for long stretches, replaced by dramatic dialogues and soliloquies from Ahab and other characters.

AHAB

Ahab, the *Pequod*'s obsessed captain, represents both an ancient and a quintessentially modern type of hero. Like the heroes of Greek or Shakespearean tragedy, Ahab suffers from a single fatal flaw, one he shares with such legendary characters as Oedipus and Faust. His tremendous overconfidence, or hubris, leads him to defy common sense and believe that, like a god, he can enact his will and remain immune to the forces of nature. He considers Moby Dick the embodiment of evil in the world, and he pursues the White Whale monomaniacally because he believes it his inescapable fate to destroy this evil. According to the critic M. H. Abrams, such a tragic hero "moves us to pity because, since he is not an evil man, his misfortune is greater than he deserves; but he moves us also to fear, because we recognize similar possibilities of error in our own lesser and fallible selves."

Unlike the heroes of older tragic works, however, Ahab suffers from a fatal flaw that is not necessarily inborn but instead stems from damage, in his case both psychological and physical, inflicted by life in a harsh world. He is as much a victim as he is an aggressor, and the symbolic opposition that he constructs between himself and Moby Dick propels him toward what he considers a destined end.

MOBY DICK

In a sense, Moby Dick is not a character, as the reader has no access to the White Whale's thoughts, feelings, or intentions. Instead, Moby Dick is an impersonal force, one that many critics have interpreted as an allegorical representation of God, an inscrutable and all-powerful being that humankind can neither understand nor defy. Moby Dick thwarts free will and cannot be defeated, only accommodated or avoided. Ishmael tries a plethora of approaches to describe whales in general, but none proves adequate. Indeed, as Ishmael points out, the majority of a whale is hidden from view at all times. In this way, a whale mirrors its environment. Like the whale, only the surface of the ocean is available for human observation and interpretation, while its depths conceal unknown and unknowable truths. Furthermore, even when Ishmael does get his hands on a "whole" whale, he is unable to determine which part—the skeleton, the head, the skin—offers the best understanding of the whole living, breathing creature; he cannot localize the essence of the whale. This conundrum can be read as a metaphor for the human relationship with the Christian God (or any other god, for that matter): God is unknowable and cannot be pinned down.

STARBUCK, STUBB, AND FLASK

The *Pequod*'s three mates are used primarily to provide philosophical contrasts with Ahab. Starbuck, the first mate, is a religious man. Sober and conservative, he relies on his Christian faith to determine

CHARACTER ANALYSIS

his actions and interpretations of events. Stubb, the second mate, is jolly and cool in moments of crisis. He has worked in the dangerous occupation of whaling for so long that the possibility of death has ceased to concern him. A fatalist, he believes that things happen as they are meant to and that there is little that he can do about it. Flask simply enjoys the thrill of the hunt and takes pride in killing whales. He doesn't stop to consider consequences at all and is "utterly lost. . . to all sense of reverence" for the whale. All three of these perspectives are used to accentuate Ahab's monomania. Ahab reads his experiences as the result of a conspiracy against him by some larger force. Unlike Flask, he thinks and interprets. Unlike Stubb, he believes that he can alter his world. Unlike Starbuck, he places himself rather than some external set of principles at the center of the cosmic order that he discerns.

THEMES, MOTIFS & SYMBOLS

THEMES

Themes are the fundamental and often universal ideas explored in a literary work.

THE LIMITS OF KNOWLEDGE

As Ishmael tries, in the opening pages of *Moby-Dick,* to offer a simple collection of literary excerpts mentioning whales, he discovers that, throughout history, the whale has taken on an incredible multiplicity of meanings. Over the course of the novel, he makes use of nearly every discipline known to man in his attempts to understand the essential nature of the whale. Each of these systems of knowledge, however, including art, taxonomy, and phrenology, fails to give an adequate account. The multiplicity of approaches that Ishmael takes, coupled with his compulsive need to assert his authority as a narrator and the frequent references to the limits of observation (men cannot see the depths of the ocean, for example), suggest that human knowledge is always limited and insufficient. When it comes to Moby Dick himself, this limitation takes on allegorical significance. The ways of Moby Dick, like those of the Christian God, are unknowable to man, and thus trying to interpret them, as Ahab does, is inevitably futile and often fatal.

THE DECEPTIVENESS OF FATE

In addition to highlighting many portentous or foreshadowing events, Ishmael's narrative contains many references to fate, creating the impression that the *Pequod*'s doom is inevitable. Many of the sailors believe in prophecies, and some even claim the ability to foretell the future. A number of things suggest, however, that characters are actually deluding themselves when they think that they see the work of fate and that fate either doesn't exist or is one of the many forces about which human beings can have no distinct knowledge. Ahab, for example, clearly exploits the sailors' belief in fate to manipulate them into thinking that the quest for Moby Dick is their common destiny. Moreover, the prophesies of Fedallah and others seem to be undercut in Chapter 99, when various individuals interpret the doubloon in different ways, demonstrating that humans project what they want to see when they try to interpret signs and portents.

THE EXPLOITATIVE NATURE OF WHALING

At first glance, the *Pequod* seems like an island of equality and fellowship in the midst of a racist, hierarchically structured world. The ship's crew includes men from all corners of the globe and all races who seem to get along harmoniously. Ishmael is initially uneasy upon meeting Queequeg, but he quickly realizes that it is better to have a "sober cannibal than a drunken Christian" for a shipmate. Additionally, the conditions of work aboard the *Pequod* promote a certain kind of egalitarianism, since men are promoted and paid according to their skill. However, the work of whaling parallels the other exploitative activities—buffalo hunting, gold mining, unfair trade with indigenous peoples—that characterize American and European territorial expansion. Each of the *Pequod*'s mates, who are white, is entirely dependent on a nonwhite harpooner, and nonwhites perform most of the dirty or dangerous jobs aboard the ship. Flask actually stands on Daggoo, his African harpooner, in order to beat the other mates to a prize whale. Ahab is depicted as walking over the black youth Pip, who listens to Ahab's pacing from below deck, and is thus reminded that his value as a slave is less than the value of a whale.

MOTIFS

Motifs are recurring structures, contrasts, or literary devices that can help to develop and inform the text's major themes.

WHITENESS

Whiteness, to Ishmael, is horrible because it represents the unnatural and threatening: albinos, creatures that live in extreme and inhospitable environments, waves breaking against rocks. These examples reverse the traditional association of whiteness with purity. Whiteness conveys both a lack of meaning and an unreadable excess of meaning that confounds individuals. Moby Dick is the pinnacle of whiteness, and Melville's characters cannot objectively understand the White Whale. Ahab, for instance, believes that Moby Dick represents evil, while Ishmael fails in his attempts to determine scientifically the whale's fundamental nature.

SURFACES AND DEPTHS

Ishmael frequently bemoans the impossibility of examining anything in its entirety, noting that only the surfaces of objects and environments are available to the human observer. On a live whale, for example, only the outer layer presents itself; on a dead whale, it is impossible to determine what constitutes the whale's skin, or which part—skeleton, blubber, head—offers the best understanding of the entire animal. Moreover, as the whale swims, it hides much of its body underwater, away from the human gaze, and no one knows where it goes or what it does. The sea itself is the greatest frustration in this regard: its depths are mysterious and inaccessible to Ishmael. This motif represents the larger problem of the limitations of human knowledge. Humankind is not all-seeing; we can only observe, and thus only acquire knowledge about, that fraction of entities—both individuals and environments—to which we have access: surfaces.

SYMBOLS

Symbols are objects, characters, figures, or colors used to represent abstract ideas or concepts.

THE PEQUOD

Named after a Native American tribe in Massachusetts that did not long survive the arrival of white men and thus memorializing an extinction, the *Pequod* is a symbol of doom. It is painted a gloomy black and covered in whale teeth and bones, literally bristling with the mementos of violent death. It is, in fact, marked for death. Adorned like a primitive coffin, the *Pequod* becomes one.

MOBY DICK

Moby Dick possesses various symbolic meanings for various individuals. To the *Pequod*'s crew, the legendary White Whale is a concept onto which they can displace their anxieties about their dangerous and often very frightening jobs. Because they have no delusions about Moby Dick acting malevolently toward men or literally embodying evil, tales about the whale allow them to confront their fear, manage it, and continue to function. Ahab, on the other hand, believes that Moby Dick is a manifestation of all that is wrong with the world, and he feels that it is his destiny to eradicate this symbolic evil.

SYMBOLS

Moby Dick also bears out interpretations not tied down to specific characters. In its inscrutable silence and mysterious habits, for example, the White Whale can be read as an allegorical representation of an unknowable God. As a profitable commodity, it fits into the scheme of white economic expansion and exploitation in the nineteenth century. As a part of the natural world, it represents the destruction of the environment by such hubristic expansion.

QUEEQUEG'S COFFIN

Queequeg's coffin alternately symbolizes life and death. Queequeg has it built when he is seriously ill, but when he recovers, it becomes a chest to hold his belongings and an emblem of his will to live. He perpetuates the knowledge tattooed on his body by carving it onto the coffin's lid. The coffin further comes to symbolize life, in a morbid way, when it replaces the *Pequod*'s life buoy. When the *Pequod* sinks, the coffin becomes Ishmael's buoy, saving not only his life but the life of the narrative that he will pass on.

Summary & Analysis

Etymology & Extracts

Etymology

Moby-Dick begins with the etymological derivation of the word "whale." Before presenting this etymology, the narrator presents the person who prepared the etymology, "a late consumptive usher to a grammar school," a sort of failed schoolmaster who occupies himself with dusting off his old books. The etymology itself offers a quotation from the sixteenth-century explorer Hackluyt that emphasizes the importance of the unpronounced "h" in "whale." One dictionary claims that the word derives from *hval*, the Swedish and Danish word for roundness, another that it derives from *Wallen*, the Dutch and German word verb meaning "to roll." These etymologies are followed by the word for whale in thirteen other languages.

Extracts

The "extracts" are quotations from various sources in which whales are mentioned. Again the narrator presents an obscure functionary as the compiler of the section, a "sub-sub-librarian." The extracts range from biblical passages to lines from Shakespeare and Dryden to descriptions from scientific treatises, explorers' accounts, and popular literature. They are numerous and suggest the wide range of things that the whale has represented at different times.

Analysis: Etymology & Extracts

By commencing with scholarly materials—an etymology and extracts from other texts—Melville indicates that *Moby-Dick* will be more than a mere adventure novel. The introductory materials suggest not only that the novel is based on a thorough study of humankind's attempts to understand the whale but that it will even attempt to make a serious contribution to this body of knowledge. Moreover, the range and variety of extracts and the canonical status of some of them suggest that whales are much more important to Western culture than people generally recognize.

The extracts are bewildering because of their variety as well as their sheer number. Novels are often prefaced with a single epigraph suggesting the central theme of the text to come and providing the reader with a point of departure. *Moby-Dick*'s extracts range from the highbrow to the lowbrow, the literary to the nonliterary, making it difficult to isolate any particular theme as central. One thing that the extracts clearly do is display the novel's commitment to intertextuality (the referencing of other literary works), which might be seen as Melville's strategy for establishing the literary worthiness of *Moby-Dick* in particular and American literature in general. The extracts imply that *Moby-Dick* is grand enough to encompass and build upon all of the works quoted here, from literary masterpieces such as Shakespeare's plays and *Paradise Lost* to works of natural science. Moreover, the collection of extracts underscores the novel's ambition to deal with a variety of human experiences, from those as profound and fundamental as the fall of man to those as mundane as schoolbooks and sensationalized magazine articles.

The consumptive usher and the "poor devil of a Sub-Sub" to whom Melville gives credit for the etymology and the excerpts add an air of pathetic comedy to the proceedings. They are stand-ins for all men, constantly struggling and seeking greatness but just as constantly overwhelmed and doomed to mediocrity. As caricatures of failed scholars, these figures lend an ironic tone to the novel's academic pretensions, possibly suggesting the essential futility of attempts to capture the meaning of the whale in words. The valor, however, is in the effort, and it is in this spirit of self-deprecation that Melville begins his novel.

CHAPTERS 1–9

CHAPTER 1: LOOMINGS
The narrative of *Moby-Dick* begins with the famous brief sentence, "Call me Ishmael." Ishmael, a sailor, describes a typical scene in New York City, with large groups of men gathering on their days off to contemplate the ocean and dream of a life at sea. He explains that he himself went to sea because, like these men, he was feeling a "damp, drizzly November in [his] soul" and craved adventure. Shunning anything too "respectable" (or expensive), he always ships as a common sailor rather than as a passenger.

CHAPTER 2: THE CARPET-BAG
Ishmael travels from New York to New Bedford, Massachusetts, the whaling capital of the United States. He arrives too late to catch the ferry to Nantucket, the original whaling center of New England;

for the sake of tradition, Ishmael wants to sail in a Nantucket whaler. For now, however, he has to spend a few nights in New Bedford. He roams the streets looking for an inn, but those that he finds seem too expensive. He stumbles into, then quickly out of, a church full of wailing and weeping African Americans, where a sermon is being preached on "the blackness of darkness." Ishmael finally wanders into the Spouter-Inn, owned by Peter Coffin. The ominous name of the inn and the owner satisfy his mood, and the place is dilapidated and sure to be cheap.

CHAPTER 3: THE SPOUTER-INN

Inside the Spouter-Inn, Ishmael finds a large, somewhat inscrutable oil painting, which he finally determines to be a depiction of a whale attacking a ship. On the other wall is a collection of "monstrous clubs and spears." Because the inn is nearly full, Ishmael learns that he will have to share a room with "a dark complexioned" harpooner named Queequeg. He passes the evening in the bar with "a wild set of mariners," waiting for Queequeg to arrive. Out of apprehension, Ishmael decides that he would rather sleep on a bench than share a bed with some strange, possibly dangerous man. The bench is too uncomfortable, though, and Ishmael decides to put up with the unknown harpooner, who, Coffin had assured him, is perfectly fine because "he pays reg'lar." Still, Ishmael is worried, since Coffin adds that the harpooner has recently arrived from the South Seas and is currently out peddling shrunken heads. When Queequeg finally returns, the frightened Ishmael watches him from the bed, noting with horror the harpooner's tattoos and tomahawk pipe. Queequeg sets up and worships a small, dark-colored idol. His prayers over, he discovers Ishmael in his bed. He flourishes the tomahawk pipe as Ishmael shouts for the inn's owner. After Coffin explains the situation, Ishmael and Queequeg settle in for the night, Ishmael having decided that it is better to share a bed with a "sober cannibal" than a "drunken Christian."

CHAPTER 4: THE COUNTERPANE

When Queequeg and Ishmael wake up the next morning, Queequeg's arm lies affectionately thrown over Ishmael, as if the latter were "his wife." Ishmael watches the cannibal don a fancy hat and boots and shave himself with his harpoon. He marvels at the "savage's understanding of civilized manners.

CHAPTER 5: BREAKFAST

The Spouter-Inn's breakfast table is filled with whalers, yet the meal, to Ishmael's surprise, is not enlivened with sea stories or bawdiness. Instead, the men eat in silence. Queequeg uses his harpoon to help himself to more meat.

CHAPTER 6: THE STREET

Ishmael wanders about New Bedford, marveling at the town and its people. Because of the maritime industry centered here, the town is full of men from all corners of the globe, from the South Pacific to the remote mountains of Vermont. The great mansions and finely dressed women of the town all exist thanks to the high prices that whale oil commands.

CHAPTER 7: THE CHAPEL

Ishmael finds the Whaleman's Chapel, which contains plaques commemorating those lost or killed at sea. He ponders the contradictory message inherent in the chapel: if heaven really is a better place, it doesn't make sense for a dead man's friends and relatives to mourn him so inconsolably. Ishmael is surprised to find Queequeg in the chapel.

CHAPTER 8: THE PULPIT

A man arrives at the chapel and climbs up a rope ladder into the pulpit, which is shaped like a ship's bow. He is Father Mapple, the preacher in this chapel, a favorite among whalemen for his sincerity and ability to make his sermons relevant to their lives. Ishmael wonders about the symbolic significance of Mapple's dramatic climb into the pulpit.

CHAPTER 9: THE SERMON

Mapple takes his theme for this Sunday's sermon from the story of Jonah, the prophet swallowed by "a great fish"—in other words, a whale. Mapple, typically, uses Jonah's story to preach about man's sin and his willful disobeying of God's commandments. But, Mapple claims, the story also speaks to him personally, urging him to fulfill God's will by "preach[ing] the Truth in the face of Falsehood!" Drained by his emotional sermon, Mapple ends kneeling, his face covering his hands, as the crowd files out.

ANALYSIS: CHAPTERS 1–9

These chapters establish the basic plot and thematic conflicts of *Moby-Dick* and also introduce two of the novel's most important characters, Queequeg and Ishmael, the latter of whom is the novel's narrator. The enigmatic command "Call me Ishmael" lends a mysteriousness to the narrator's identity; nevertheless, his seemingly adopted name signals his identification with the biblical outcast from the Book of Genesis. One of the first things we learn about Ishmael is that he is going to sea as a sort of self-annihilation—an alternative to "throw[ing] himself upon his sword." Ishmael is a dreamer, given to philosophical speculation, but essentially passive. He is more of an observer than a major participant.

Although it is not apparent from the novel's first chapter, Ishmael is more than just the narrator. His remarks later in the novel indicate that he has produced the text that we have in our hands and that the extracts and scholarly materials that preface the book are the fruits of his own researches. From the outset of his narrative, there is a marked difference between Ishmael's low status as a character, in which role he is a nearly penniless and inexperienced junior hand on board ship, and his magisterial presence as a narrator, with his sweeping philosophical and scientific ambitions. Clearly, he writes as a much older and more experienced sailor than he is during the events of the novel.

Ishmael's lengthy and speculative digressions suggest that the things he observes have metaphorical significance, but it is often difficult to discern what specific things signify: even Ishmael himself seems to be uncertain in this regard. Father Mapple's elaborate pulpit, for example, appears to have a symbolic meaning, but Ishmael admits that he cannot quite figure out what it is. The painting on the wall of the Spouter-Inn is so dark and dirty that it is almost impossible to make out its subject, and Ishmael offers several alternatives for what it may depict. In the end, he determines that it shows a whale attacking a ship and impaling itself upon the ship's masts. This interpretation, however, doesn't seem particularly realistic, and offers more confusion than clarity.

The two churches that Ishmael enters in these chapters suggest two distinct religious attitudes. The sermon preached in the black church is on "the blackness of darkness," suggesting that evil is impenetrable and cannot be understood by human beings. Father Mapple's sermon about Jonah demands that people heed God's call and proclaim the truth even in the face of great hostility, even when that truth goes against conventional ways of thinking. While the first sermon exemplifies the belief that the human being's power of understanding truth is extremely limited, the second suggests that God gives humans the power to apprehend truth, and that men and women should be so confident in their vision of this truth as to defy any opposition. Throughout Ishmael's narrative, these two interpretations of human understanding vie with one another for primacy.

The comical process by which Ishmael befriends Queequeg introduces one of the novel's major facets: the topic of race relations. By developing a relationship with this "savage," Ishmael shows that he isn't bound by his prejudices. Indeed, his interactions with Queequeg make Ishmael realize that although most would call Queequeg a savage, the harpooner actually has a deeper understanding of what "civilization" means than most whites do, as his grooming habits demonstrate. Realizing that Queequeg treats him "with so much civility and consideration" while he himself was "guilty of great rudeness," Ishmael reexamines stereotypes about so-called savages. In fact, "for all his tattooings," says Ishmael, Queequeg "was on the whole a clean, comely looking cannibal." Queequeg's tattoos and supposed cannibalism mark him, in terms of nineteenth-century beliefs, as the ultimate savage. Tattooing is a voluntary alteration of the body that, unlike a hairstyle or clothing choice, is permanent; cannibalism is another fundamental Western taboo. Beyond these two characteristics, Queequeg is a veritable melting pot of different racial and ethnic traits: African, Polynesian, Islamic, Christian, and Native American. Allegedly from Kokovoko, an island in the South Seas, he worships an idol that looks like "a three days' old Congo baby" (West African) in a Ramadan (Islamic) ceremony and carries a tomahawk pipe (North American indigenous tribal).

CHAPTERS 10–21

CHAPTER 10: A BOSOM FRIEND

> *Thus, then, in our hearts' honeymoon, lay I and*
> *Queequeg—a cosy, loving pair.*
> *(See* QUOTATIONS, *p. 73)*

Contemplating Queequeg's serene comportment, Ishmael develops a great respect for his new friend, noting that "[y]ou cannot hide the soul" under tattoos and appearances. Although Ishmael still thinks of Queequeg as a savage, the latter becomes, in Ishmael's mind, "George Washington cannibalistically developed." Ishmael makes some small gestures of friendship toward Queequeg, and the two become friendly. He admires Queequeg's sincerity and lack of Chris-

tian "hollow courtesies." According to the customs of Queequeg's
home, he and Queequeg are "married" after a social smoke out of
the tomahawk pipe. Queequeg gives Ishmael half his belongings,
and the two continue to share a bed, having many long chats. Ishmael even consents to join in Queequeg's idol worship, explaining
to his Christian readers that he is only obeying the Golden Rule, as
he would hope the "savage" to join in Christian worship with him.

CHAPTER 11: NIGHTGOWN
Queequeg and Ishmael awaken in the middle of the night. It is cold
and the warmth of the bed and of their companionship is pleasant.
They share a smoke, and Queequeg begins to recount his life story.

CHAPTER 12: BIOGRAPHICAL
Queequeg is a native of a South Pacific island called Kokovoko,
which is "not down on any map; true places never are." The king's
son, he desired to leave the island to see the world and, he claims, to
learn about Christianity. When a whaling ship stopped at Kokovoko, he sought passage but was denied a job. He stowed away on
the departing ship and, through sheer persistence, was finally taken
on as a whaler. He has since become a skilled harpooner. Although
his father is probably dead by now, meaning that Queequeg would
be king, he can never go back, because his interaction with Christianity has made him unfit to ascend his homeland's "pure and
undefiled throne." For Queequeg, Ishmael notes, "that barbed iron
[Queequeg's harpoon] was in lieu of a scepter now." The two plan to
go to Nantucket to find a berth aboard a whaler.

CHAPTER 13: WHEELBARROW
Together, Ishmael and Queequeg set off for Nantucket with a wheel-
barrow full of their things. The people of New Bedford stare at this
white man and "savage" behaving so friendly with each other. Queequeg tells Ishmael stories about the first time that he used a wheel-
barrow (he picked it up instead of wheeling it) and about a white
captain who attended a wedding feast on Kokovoko and made a
fool of himself. On the ferry to Nantucket, a bumpkin mimics Queequeg. Queequeg flips the man around in the air to rebuke him and
is subsequently scolded by the captain. A moment later, a rope in the
ferry's rigging breaks, and the bumpkin is swept overboard as the
ferry goes out of control. Queequeg takes charge of the ropes to
secure the ferry and then dives into the water to save the man who
has gone overboard, which wins everyone's respect.

CHAPTER 14: NANTUCKET
Ishmael digresses from the story to discuss the island of Nantucket. He details some of the legends about its founding and some of the tall tales that are told about life on the island. He notes that a Nantucketer "owns" the seas and that this "empire," covering two-thirds of the globe, is larger than that of any country.

CHAPTER 15: CHOWDER
Ishmael and Queequeg settle at the Try-Pots for the night, an inn owned by the cousin of the Spouter-Inn's owner. Ishmael is disturbed by an old topmast above the inn that looks ominously like a gallows. Everything on Nantucket is touched by the sea: the milk tastes of fish, and the innkeeper's wife wears a necklace of fish vertebrae. The two friends have a supper of hearty chowder.

CHAPTER 16: THE SHIP
Charged by Yojo, Queequeg's wooden idol, to seek a ship for the two men, Ishmael lights upon the *Pequod,* a ship "with an old fashioned claw-footed look about her" and "apparelled like any barbaric Ethiopian emperor, his neck heavy with pendants of polished ivory." Ishmael also calls the *Pequod* a "cannibal of a craft" because it is bejeweled with whale parts. On board, he makes a deal with Peleg and Bildad, the ship's Quaker owners, who are characterized as conniving cheapskates and bitter taskmasters. Although Quakers are generally pacifists, these two have dedicated their life to the bloody slaughter of whales. Evaluating what lay Ishmael should receive (his portion of the ship's profits and his only wages), Peleg finally gives him the 300th lay. At this time, Ishmael also learns that the ship's captain is the mysterious Ahab, named after a wicked biblical king. Although Ahab has been moody and secretive since losing his leg in an encounter with the great white whale Moby Dick, Bildad and Peleg believe in his competence and they believe him harmless, since he has a young wife and an infant child waiting for him at home.

CHAPTER 17: THE RAMADAN
Returning to the inn, Ishmael allows Queequeg a day for his "Ramadan" ceremonies and then worries when his friend doesn't answer the door in the evening. When the panicky Ishmael finally gets the door open, he finds Queequeg deep in meditation. Queequeg is unresponsive and continues to meditate until the next morning. Ishmael talks to Queequeg about the discomforts of Queequeg's religion. The next day, after a large breakfast, they return to the *Pequod.*

CHAPTER 18: HIS MARK
Though the owners object at first to his paganism, Queequeg impresses them with his skill by hitting a tiny spot of tar on the water with a harpoon. They give him the ninetieth lay, "more than ever was given a harpooneer yet out of Nantucket." Bildad tries to convert Queequeg to Christianity, but Peleg tells him to give up: "Pious harpooneers never make good voyagers—it takes the shark out of 'em; no harpooneer is worth a straw who ain't pretty sharkish." Peleg reminds Bildad that, at sea, practical concerns shove religious matters aside.

CHAPTER 19: THE PROPHET
Just after signing the papers, Ishmael and Queequeg run into a scarred and deformed man named Elijah, a prophet or perhaps merely a frightening stranger, who hints to them about the peril of signing aboard Ahab's ship. He drops references to several frightening incidents involving Ahab, but Ishmael and Queequeg disregard the man's warnings.

CHAPTER 20: ALL ASTIR
Over the course of several days, the ship is provisioned for the coming voyage. Ishmael hears that Ahab's health is improving—he is still recovering from the loss of his leg—but he and Queequeg have yet to meet the mysterious captain.

CHAPTER 21: GOING ABOARD
Approaching the *Pequod* at dawn, Ishmael thinks that he sees sailors boarding the ship and decides that the ship must be leaving at sunrise. Ishmael and Queequeg encounter Elijah again just before they board. Elijah asks Ishmael whether he saw "anything looking like men" boarding the ship; Ishmael replies that he did. The ship, however, is quiet save one old sailor, who informs them that the captain is already aboard. As the sun rises, the *Pequod*'s crew arrives and the ship prepares to sail.

ANALYSIS: CHAPTERS 10–21
In these chapters, a remarkably intense bond develops between Ishmael and Queequeg. Ishmael progresses from seeing Queequeg as a thing "hideously marred" about the face and body with tattoos to comparing Queequeg to George Washington. The two become "a cosy, loving pair" and exemplify an ideal friendship based on respect and sharing. The citizens of New Bedford, though used to

seeing cannibals in their streets, are shocked by the pair's closeness, and many of Ishmael's comments about Queequeg are calculated to shock the nineteenth-century reader. Ishmael's blithe acceptance and even embracing of Queequeg's idolatry is a prime example of Melville's attempt to provoke a reaction. Though he acknowledges that he is a Presbyterian, Ishmael refuses to insist on the correctness of his own religion, instead focusing on the unity of religions and the brotherhood of man.

Ishmael's narrative continues to cast doubt on prejudice and dogma, both racial and religious. Ironically, Queequeg views his exposure to Christians as a contaminant that makes him unfit to rule his native people rather than a benefit or deliverance from ignorance. He disproves the prejudice of the Nantucket ferry's passengers and captain by saving the ferry and the bumpkin who goes overboard, demonstrating that he is not a dangerous "devil." His skill with a harpoon persuades Peleg and Bildad to ignore his religious practices and give him a berth on the *Pequod*. Though a Quaker, Peleg admits that religious principles are of little use at sea, where daring and attention to the tasks at hand are necessary for survival. There are limits, however, to Ishmael's tolerance. Queequeg's extreme abstinence during his "Ramadan" ritual provokes Ishmael to remonstrate with him—to no avail—about the folly of religious "dyspepsia," referring to the malnourishment that he believes results from fasting.

These chapters are filled with foreshadowing and dark imagery. Elijah, who shares his name with the Old Testament prophet who foretold destruction to the biblical Ahab, tells Ishmael and Queequeg that the *Pequod* is doomed. Indeed, the ship itself is an emblem of death. Named after a tribe of New England Indians killed off by white settlers, it is covered in whale bones and teeth and cloaked in dark paint. Elijah's fears seem to have some basis in fact, as he refers to incidents of bad judgment and unnecessary risk involving Ahab. Ahab himself, "desperate moody, and savage," inspires sympathy, pity, and "a strange awe" in Ishmael. Named for the Israelite king who angers God with his worship of idols, Ahab seems an ominous figure. His obsession with the whale—a sort of perverse worship—has already injured him corporeally and spiritually, and we sense that the conflict will only heighten.

CHAPTERS 22-31

CHAPTER 22: MERRY CHRISTMAS
The *Pequod* leaves Nantucket on a cold Christmas Day. Bildad and Peleg pilot the ship out of port. Ahab still has not appeared on deck. Ishmael finds the start of the voyage disconcerting and is meditating upon his situation when he receives a kick and a scolding from Peleg. The *Pequod* is soon clear of the harbor and into the open ocean, and Bildad and Peleg take a small boat back to shore as the whaling ship "plunge[s] like fate into the lone Atlantic."

CHAPTER 23: THE LEE SHORE
Ishmael offers a brief portrait of Bulkington, a sailor whom he first meets in New Bedford. Ishmael watches Bulkington steer the *Pequod* and thinks of him as a restless pioneer, fated to die at sea. Ishmael considers this kind of death infinitely preferable to fading away through cowardice, and, in an imaginary address to Bulkington, declares that the death at sea will transform Bulkington into a god.

CHAPTER 24: THE ADVOCATE
Ishmael proceeds to stand up for the whaling profession, arguing that whaling is heroic, economically critical, and has expanded geographical knowledge. He defends the dignity of whaling by pointing to the involvement of noble families in the industry, to the fact that the Bible and other books mention whales, and to the fact that Cetus, the whale, is a constellation in the southern sky. Ishmael closes by declaring that anything worthwhile that he might accomplish can be credited to his time spent on a whaling ship, his "Yale College" and his "Harvard."

CHAPTER 25: POSTSCRIPT
Ishmael adds some speculation to the previous chapter's "facts." He reminds the reader that sperm whale oil is used in the coronation of royalty, and suggests that sperm oil has been used to anoint kings because it is the best, purest, and sweetest of oils.

CHAPTER 26: KNIGHTS AND SQUIRES
In the first of the two chapters called "Knights and Squires," we meet the first mate, Starbuck, a pragmatic, reliable Nantucketer. Starbuck believes that it is rational—and necessary—to fear whales, and his reverence for nature inclines him toward superstition. He is characterized by the other officers of the *Pequod* as "careful,"

although this term is relative when used to describe a whaler. Speaking about Starbuck leads Ishmael to reflect upon the dignity of the working man. Ishmael finds evidence of God in even the "meanest mariners" and admits that he will frequently ignore people's faults to emphasize their "democratic dignity."

CHAPTER 27: KNIGHTS AND SQUIRES

This chapter introduces the rest of the *Pequod*'s officers. The pipe-smoking second mate, Stubb, a native of Cape Cod, is always cool under pressure and possesses "impious good humor." The third mate, Flask, a native of Tisbury on Martha's Vineyard, is a short, stocky fellow with a confrontational attitude and no reverence for the dignity of the whale. He is nicknamed "King-Post" because he resembles the short, square timber known by that name in Arctic whalers. Each mate commands one of the small harpoon boats that are sent out after whales, and each has a "squire," his harpooner: Queequeg is Starbuck's harpooner; Tashtego, "an unmixed Indian from Gay Head," on Martha's Vineyard, is Stubb's harpooner; and Daggoo, "a gigantic, coal-black negro-savage" from Africa with an imperial bearing, is Flask's harpooner.

Ishmael notes that few whalers are American-born except the officers, who are almost always American: "the native American liberally provides the brains, the rest of the world as generously supplies the muscles." The rest of the crew is also international. But, says Ishmael, all of these "Isolatoes" are "federated along one keel" and unified by their comradeship at sea and shared danger. Ishmael also mentions Pip, a poor black boy from Alabama who beats a tambourine on ship.

CHAPTER 28: AHAB

As the *Pequod* ranges further south and the weather improves, Ahab finally appears on deck. Ishmael observes him closely. Ahab appears a strong, willful figure, though his encounter with Moby Dick has scarred him both physically and mentally. In addition to missing a leg, Ahab is marked with a white scar down one side of his face that looks like a lightning strike. Rumor has it that the scar suddenly appeared during some "elemental strife at sea." Ahab stands watch with his false leg, carved from a whale's jaw, set into a hole bored into the deck.

CHAPTER 29: ENTER AHAB; TO HIM, STUBB

Ahab does indeed seem psychologically troubled. He maintains a total dictatorship on board. He is restless and paces the deck, and the striking of his peg leg on the wood echoes throughout the ship. When Stubb complains about Ahab's pacing, Ahab calls him a dog and advances on him. Stubb retreats. This chapter is short and dramatic, as the stage-direction title implies.

CHAPTER 30: THE PIPE
Ahab realizes that smoking no longer soothes him and that the sereneness of the activity doesn't suit his agitated, willful state of mind. He hurls his pipe overboard and resumes pacing the ship deck.

CHAPTER 31: QUEEN MAB
The next morning, Stubb tells Flask that he dreamed that Ahab kicked him with his ivory leg. An old merman in the dream points out the futility of struggling against Ahab and suggests that it may even be an honor to be kicked by such a man. (The title of this chapter, "Queen Mab," refers to Shakespeare's tragedy *Romeo and Juliet,* in which Mercutio explains how Queen Mab, a fairy, brings dreams to sleepers.) As Stubb finishes telling of his dream, Ahab shouts at the crew to be on the lookout for whales. The *Pequod*'s work has begun.

ANALYSIS: CHAPTERS 22–31
These chapters introduce the other men aboard the ship and begin to describe the onboard dynamics. The disparate nature of the crew, composed of men from various nations, doesn't prevent the ship from functioning properly. The sense of harmony on the *Pequod* is quite different from the racially divided nineteenth-century American society on land. The leadership structure of the ship is, however, divided by color: the officers are white and the sailors are from the South Sea Islands, Gay Head, Africa, and other far corners of the globe. Ishmael's offhand remark that Americans provide the "brains" and the rest of the world the "muscle" for this undertaking and many others reveals his belief in the harmony of such an arrangement.

Critic Alan Heimert has suggested that the pairing of mates and harpooners mirrors relationships of oppression in the nineteenth century. Starbuck represents New England and, just as this region depends on the Chinese/South Sea trade, he depends on Queequeg. Stubb represents the American West, and his power derives from his subordination of the Native American Indian, Tashtego. Flask represents the South and both controls and depends upon the African, Daggoo. While these pairings do reflect larger social structures, however, they also involve relationships that are much more complicated and much more interdependent than simple master-slave or boss-worker exchanges. The *Pequod* depends on cooperation for success in catching whales and sometimes for mere survival at sea, and men, in the end, are assessed according to their skill rather than race. Melville explores the development of an alternative, more egalitarian social system aboard the ship throughout *Moby-Dick*. At this point, the irresistibly charismatic Ahab rules the ship. "[M]oody stricken Ahab [stands] before [his crew] with a crucifixion in his face"; he clearly represents a force that will not be denied. Obedience is crucial to maintaining onboard discipline and the chain of command, and captains were allowed and even expected to be tyrants. The suggestion, in Stubb's dream, that one should consider it a privilege to be abused by Ahab rationalizes his despotism and hints at the grandiose folly in which the sailors will soon become entangled.

These chapters illustrate Ishmael's peculiar style of narration. The chronological, plot-driven story is interwoven with digressions, character sketches, and rhetorical exercises. Some chapters, like Chapter 29, are presented as if they were scenes in a play. Ishmael is also given to foreboding language and foreshadowing: the *Pequod* "plunge[s] like fate," Ahab has a "crucifixion in his face," and Stubb speaks of something strange going on in the hold. The events that unfold are meant to seem like the fulfillment of Ahab's destiny and the natural consequence of his megalomaniacal behavior. Ishmael constructs his narrative to suggest and anticipate what will happen rather than to create the effect of surprise.

CHAPTERS 32–40

CHAPTER 32: CETOLOGY

"Cetology," as Ishmael explains, is "the science of whales." In this and subsequent science-centered chapters in the book, Ishmael attempts to classify whales scientifically. He includes quotations from various writings on the whale, adding that others might be able to revise this draft of a classification system. Rather than using the Linnaean classifications of family, genus, and species—which were already the standard in Melville's time—Ishmael divides whales into different "chapters" of three distinct "books": the Folio, Octavo, and Duodecimo.

CHAPTER 33: THE SPECKSYNDER

"The Specksynder" resembles the previous chapter, but it analyzes the whaling industry rather than whales. Beginning with trivia about the changing role of the specksynder (literally, "fat-cutter"), who used to be chief harpooner and captain, Ishmael moves on to a discussion of onboard leadership styles. He notes that the dependence of whalers upon one another for successful hunting and therefore wages begets its own discipline, and that a whaling ship is less hierarchical than other vessels. Nevertheless, many captains make a great show of their rank. Ahab doesn't flaunt his superiority, although he can be a tyrant. In fact, Ishmael admits that it can be hard to see exactly what is remarkable about Ahab: one must "dive . . . for [it] in the deep."

CHAPTER 34: THE CABIN-TABLE

This chapter shows the ship's officers at dinner. Meals are a rigid affair over which Ahab presides: no one talks, and a strict order of service is followed. After the officers finish eating, the table is relaid for the harpooners, who eat heartily, intimidating the cook with their voraciousness. The cabin is not a comfortable place for anyone, as it is Ahab's territory and Ahab is "inaccessible," "an alien."

CHAPTER 35: THE MAST-HEAD

Ishmael describes his first post on the masthead (the top of the ship's masts) watching for whales. He provides a history of mastheads and their role on whaling ships. He proceeds to discuss statues, hermits, and ancient Egyptians as prior "mast-head standers." The masthead is a place where whalers spend a great deal of time, and Ishmael laments its lack of comforts: on a South Seas ship, the masthead offers only two small pegs upon which to stand. He compares this setup to that of other ships, which have miniature cabins atop the masts. Ishmael admits that he himself daydreams too much to keep a good watch, and he warns captains against hiring "romantic, melancholy, and absent-minded young men," who are likely to miss whales in the vicinity.

CHAPTER 36: THE QUARTER-DECK (ENTER AHAB: THEN, ALL.)

Ahab finally makes an official appearance before the men. First, he stirs the crew by calling out simple questions about their mission, to which they respond in unison. He then presents a Spanish gold doubloon, proclaiming, "Whosoever of ye raises me a white-headed whale with a wrinkled brow and a crooked jaw . . . he shall have this gold ounce, my boys!" The men cheer, and the harpooners ask if it is Moby Dick that Ahab seeks. Ahab then confesses, in response to Starbuck's query, that it was indeed Moby Dick who stripped him of his leg, and he announces his quest to hunt the whale down. The men shout together that they will hunt with Ahab, though Starbuck protests that he "came here to hunt whales, not [his] commander's vengeance." Ahab commences a ritual that binds the crew together: he orders all of his men to drink from one flagon that gets passed around. Telling the harpooners to cross their lances before him, Ahab grasps the weapons and anoints Queequeg, Tashtego, and Daggoo "my three pagan kinsmen there—yon three most honorable gentlemen and noble men." He then makes them take the iron off of the harpoons to use as drinking goblets. They all drink together as Ahab proclaims, "God hunt us all, if we do not hunt Moby Dick to his death!"

CHAPTER 37: SUNSET

Over unsounded gorges, through the rifled hearts of
mountains, under torrents' beds, unerringly I rush!
(See QUOTATIONS, *p. 74)*

"Sunset" begins with a stage direction that sets Ahab alone near a window and consists of a melancholy soliloquy by Ahab. He notes that everyone thinks that he is mad and that he agrees with them to a certain extent. He self-consciously calls himself "demoniac" and "madness maddened." He reveals that it was foretold that he would be dismembered by a whale. He proclaims, however, that he will be both "prophet" and "fulfiller" of Moby Dick's destiny. He accepts the inequality of the battle and challenges Moby Dick, claiming that the whale cannot avoid his fate: "The path to my fixed purpose is laid with iron rails, whereon my soul is grooved to run."

CHAPTER 38: DUSK

"Dusk" is Starbuck's monologue. Though he fears that all will turn out ill, he feels inextricably bound to Ahab, compelled to help him to "his impious end." When he hears the revelry coming from the crew's forecastle, he laments the whole doomed voyage and the "latent horror" in life.

CHAPTER 39: FIRST NIGHT-WATCH

"First Night-Watch" is Stubb's monologue, providing yet another perspective on the voyage. Stubb, believing all to be "predestinated," can only laugh and sing a ditty.

CHAPTER 40: MIDNIGHT, FORECASTLE

"Midnight, Forecastle" is scripted like a scene from a play and presents the sailors, all of different nationalities, showing off and singing together. They get into a fight when a Spanish sailor makes fun of Daggoo. The onset of a storm, however, halts their fighting and makes them tend to the ship. Pip asks the "big white God," who may be either God or Ahab, to "have mercy on this small black boy."

ANALYSIS: CHAPTERS 32–40

"Cetology" seems to be a grandiose digression, a way for Ishmael to show off his knowledge and his literary bent. The use of publishing terminology (the category names Folio, Octavo, and Duodecimo come from the different sizes of books produced by nineteenth-century printers) suggests the arbitrariness of human attempts to understand and classify the natural world. For Ishmael, though, the meaning lies not in the final classification but in the act of classifying, which signifies hope and resistance to futility. The classification also suggests that humans, in their imperfection, need such aids to understanding, lest they be lost in a deep and fathomless sea of information and phenomena.

With the statement of his quest, Ahab reveals his motivation to be considerably more complicated than resentment at losing his leg. Ahab's desire to strike at the world's malevolent agency indicates his profound intelligence and the philosophical reach of his mind; he looks for hidden realities beneath superficial appearances. At the same time, his sentiments suggest delusion and madness. One of the puzzling questions presented by his soliloquy is whether God is the malevolent agency against which Ahab seeks to strike out. Ahab echoes both Hamlet, in his probing of the metaphysical truths underlying everyday appearances, and Iago, in his absolute rejection of piety and morality and his manipulation of others in pursuit of his goal. In any case, Ahab strives to exceed the limits proscribed for human beings by conventional morality and religion.

Beginning with Chapter 36, the chapters in this section feature stage directions and other devices borrowed from plays. These elements heighten the reader's awareness that the book is becoming more dramatic: conflicts emerge between the characters, and Ahab self-consciously gives a performance to unite and manipulate his crew. These chapters often echo Shakespeare, both in their general style and in specific allusions to Shakespeare's plays. Ahab's soliloquy, in particular, masterfully imitates Shakespearean cadences and rhythms. Both Ahab and Starbuck are given soliloquy-style monologues in these chapters, each getting the chance to plead his case to the audience, as it were, as eloquently as he can.

CHAPTERS 41–47

CHAPTER 41: MOBY DICK

[A]ll evil, to crazy Ahab, were visibly personified and
made practically assailable in Moby Dick.
(See QUOTATIONS, *p. 75)*

Ishmael compares the legend of Moby Dick to his experience of the whale. He notes that sperm whale attacks have increased recently and that superstitious sailors have come to regard these attacks as having an intelligent, even supernatural origin. In particular, wild rumors about Moby Dick circulate among whalemen, suggesting that he can be in more than one place at the same time and that he is immortal. Ishmael remarks that even the wildest of rumors usually contains some truth. Whales, for instance, have been known to travel with remarkable speed from the Atlantic to the Pacific; thus, it is possible for a whale to be caught in the Pacific with the harpoons of a Greenland ship in it. Moby Dick, who has defied capture numerous times, exhibits an "intelligent malignity" in his attacks on men.

Ishmael explains that Ahab lost his leg when he tried to attack Moby Dick with a knife after the whale destroyed his boats. Far from land, Ahab did not have access to much in the way of medical care and thus underwent unimaginable physical and mental suffering on the ship's return to Nantucket. Ishmael deduces that Ahab's madness and his single-minded drive to destroy the whale must have originated during his bedridden agony.

CHAPTER 42: THE WHITENESS OF THE WHALE

Ishmael explains what Moby Dick meant to him at the time of the voyage: above all, it was the whiteness of the whale that appalled him. Ishmael begins his discussion of "whiteness" by noting its use as a symbol of virtue, nobility, and racial superiority. To him, the color white only multiplies the terror when it is attached to any object already "terrible" in and of itself, such as a shark or polar bear.

CHAPTER 43: HARK!

This chapter offers a short, dramatic dialogue between two sailors on watch. One thinks that he has heard a humanlike noise from the hold (where a ship's cargo is normally stowed). The other hears nothing, and the first reminds him that Stubb and others have whispered about a mysterious passenger in the hold.

CHAPTER 44: THE CHART

Ishmael describes Ahab's attempts to locate Moby Dick. Ahab believes that he can predict where the whale will be by tracing currents that the whale might follow in search of food. He is also aware that Moby Dick has been known to show up in a certain place at the same time every year. Ahab's single-minded focus occasionally leads him to burst into fits of near-mad shrieking. Ishmael speculates that these fits are the result of the remainder of Ahab's soul trying to escape from his demented psyche.

CHAPTER 45: THE AFFIDAVIT

Ishmael acknowledges that the reader may find the story thus far presented to be incredible and cites several items from his own experience and from written authorities to bolster the probability of his narrative. First, he demonstrates the uniqueness of individual whales and the frequency with which whales survive attack by humans. He then considers why people may not believe such stories: perhaps readers haven't heard about the perils or vivid adventures common to the whaling industry. He asks that the audience use "human reasoning" when judging his story and not read it as a "hideous and intolerable allegory."

CHAPTER 46: SURMISES

Ishmael considers the means by which Ahab will exact his revenge. Because Ahab must use men as his tools, he has to be careful to maintain their loyalty throughout the long sea voyage. Ahab knows that he can appeal to their emotions for a limited time but that cash is a more reliable motivator. He is acutely aware that his behavior leaves him open to the charge of "usurpation," since he has changed the purpose of the voyage from that which the ships' owners intended. He knows that he must aggressively pursue all sperm whales in his path or his officers will have grounds to relieve him of his command.

CHAPTER 47: THE MAT-MAKER

Ishmael describes the slow, dreamy atmosphere on the ship when it is not in pursuit of a whale. He and Queequeg make a sword-mat, and Ishmael likens their weaving to work on "the Loom of Time": the threads of the warp are fixed like necessity, and man has limited free will, as he can interweave his own cross-threads into this fixed structure. When Queequeg's sword hits the loom and alters the overall pattern, Ishmael calls this chance. He is jolted out of his reverie by Tashtego's sighting of a whale. Suddenly, everyone is busied in preparation for the whale hunt. Just as the men are about to push off in the harpoon boats, "five dusky phantoms" emerge around Ahab.

ANALYSIS: CHAPTERS 42–47

These chapters contain very little action, focusing instead on the meaning of the events already described. In the first place, Ishmael takes considerable pains to ensure that the reader will not interpret his story as a tall tale fabricated to impress the gullible. He demonstrates in great detail that a specific whale can be recognized, become the subject of rumor and legend, and even be hunted. His request that his narrative be taken literally and not as some "hideous and intolerable allegory" emphasizes that Ahab's desire to kill Moby Dick exists not on some symbolic level but rather in the realm of corporeal experience.

Ishmael's protestation against allegorical interpretation is obviously ironic, since the reader knows that Ishmael's story is fiction and has witnessed Ishmael's inordinate tendency to introduce an allegorical or metaphorical aspect into almost everything that his narrative touches. But Ishmael is also in earnest, as his exhaustive presentation of facts about whales demonstrates. The point of this irony seems to be that the events of the novel were not invented by an author (whether Melville or Ishmael) in order to communicate a single allegorical meaning. Rather, the novel presents events that could, apparently, happen and explores the different ways in which people—Ahab, Ishmael, the other sailors—interpret these same events. The movements of whales, like all of the secrets of the ocean, are largely hidden, and the whalemen's struggles to piece together what they see and hear resemble other people's struggles to make meaning out of life or stories in books.

Ishmael returns repeatedly to a scientific model to interpret various phenomena. He assembles a mass of empirical observations about whales and whaling and systematizes it, modifying the work of previous naturalists and leaving behind an account that could be modified by scientists after him. Moreover, he demonstrates that records of whale sightings form the subject of a captain's practical knowledge, so that whales can be actively and methodically hunted.

The symbolic or subjective meaning of Moby Dick's existence is a more complicated matter. The rumors circulated by the whalemen about Moby Dick's ubiquity and immortality seem rooted in a credulousness born of fear and superstition. Ahab's obsession with the whale is far more profound than that of the other sailors. He projects all of his intuitions about the presence of evil in the world onto the White Whale. Though Ishmael notes the inherent absurdity of this projection, his remark that other cultures have presumed the existence of malignant forces in the world suggests that Ahab's belief in an intelligent and malignant presence lurking behind creation is not necessarily wrong.

CHAPTERS 48–54

CHAPTER 48: THE FIRST LOWERING

As the crew launches the harpoon boats for the first time this voyage, Ahab's secret crew emerges from the hold and boards the captain's harpoon boat. Fedallah, their leader, is a dark, sinister figure with a Chinese jacket and a turban made from coiling his own hair around his head. With him are several more "tiger-yellow . . . natives of the Manillas" (the Philippines) who have been hiding in the hold of the *Pequod*. Ishmael recalls the shadowy figures that he saw boarding the ship in Nantucket, the strange noises that have been heard coming from the hold, and Ahab's frequent visits down there: all these phenomena are explained by the presence of Fedallah and his men. The harpoon boat crews stare at their newly discovered shipmates, but Flask tells them to continue doing their jobs—to concentrate on hunting the whale. The *Pequod*'s first lowering after a pod of whales is unsuccessful. Flask must stand on his harpooner Daggoo's shoulders because he is too short to see otherwise. Queequeg manages to land a harpoon in a whale, but the animal overturns the boat. The men in Queequeg's boat are nearly crushed by the ship as it passes looking for them, since a squall has cast mist over everything. Finally, however, they are pulled aboard.

CHAPTER 49: THE HYENA

Ishmael laughs at the absurdity of the situation in which he finds himself: he has never been on a whaling voyage before, and he is surprised at the danger that attends even an ordinary whale hunt. The *Pequod*'s mates tell him that they have hunted whales in much more dangerous conditions than those that Ishmael has just witnessed. Ishmael decides to rewrite his will and asks Queequeg to help him do so. He feels better afterward, and comes to a morbid understanding of himself as a man already dead: any additional time that he survives at sea will be a bonus.

CHAPTER 50: AHAB'S BOAT AND CREW · FEDALLAH

Ahab's decision to have his own harpoon boat and crew, says Ishmael, is not a typical practice in the whaling industry. Captains do not frequently risk themselves in pursuit of whales, and Ahab's injury makes it even more surprising that he would personally command a harpoon boat. Clearly the *Pequod*'s owners would not approve, which accounts for Ahab's secrecy about Fedallah and his plans. However strange, "in a whaler, wonders soon wane" because there are so many unconventional sights on such a voyage. Even though whalemen are not easily awestruck, they find Ahab's crew bizarre, and "[t]hat hair-turbaned Fedallah remained a muffled mystery to the last." Ishmael hints that there is something demoniacal about the man.

CHAPTER 51: THE SPIRIT-SPOUT

Looking down from the masthead one night, Fedallah thinks that he sees a whale spouting. The ship then tries to follow it but the whale is not seen again. Mysteriously, a similar spout is seen regularly each night from then on. Ishmael calls it a "spirit-spout" because it seems to be a phantom leading them on. Some think it might be Moby Dick leading the ship on toward its destruction. The *Pequod* sails around the Cape of Good Hope at the southern tip of Africa, a particularly treacherous passage. Through it all, Ahab commands the deck robustly and, even when he is down in the cabin, keeps his eye on the cabin compass that tells him where the ship is going. Between the phantom spout and the dangerous passage, the men resign themselves to being "practical fatalists."

CHAPTER 52: THE ALBATROSS

The men soon see a ship called the *Goney*, or *Albatross*, a vessel with a "spectral appearance" that has been at sea for four years. Ahab

asks this ship's crew, as the two ships pass by, if they have seen Moby Dick. The other captain tries to respond, but a gust of wind blows the speaking trumpet from his mouth. The two ships' wakes cross as they continue on, and the schools of fish that have been following the *Pequod* turn to follow the *Albatross*, which saddens Ahab. The *Pequod* continues its way "around the world," and Ishmael ruminates that this grand-sounding mission really amounts to going in circles.

CHAPTER 53: THE GAM
Ishmael then explains why the *Pequod* and the *Albatross* did not have a "gam." Ishmael defines a gam as "*[a] social meeting of two (or more) Whale-ships, generally on a cruising-ground; when, after exchanging hails, they exchange visits by boats' crews: the two captains remaining, for the time, on board of one ship, and the two chief mates on the other.*" Ships typically exchange letters, reading material, and news of their relative successes. Ahab, however, desires gams only with ships whose captains have information about Moby Dick.

CHAPTER 54: THE TOWN-HO'S STORY (AS TOLD AT THE GOLDEN INN.)
Ishmael narrates a story about another ship, the *Town-Ho,* that was originally told to Tashtego during a gam between the *Town-Ho* and the *Pequod.* Ishmael announces at the beginning of the chapter that he gives the reader the version that he once told to some Spanish friends in Lima. The basic story concerns Radney, a mate from Martha's Vineyard, and Steelkilt, a sailor from Buffalo, who have a conflict on board the *Town-Ho,* a sperm whaler from Nantucket. Steelkilt rebels against Radney's authority, assaults him after being provoked, and starts a mutiny. The mutineers are captured, flogged, and released, but Steelkilt wants revenge against Radney, who flogged him when the captain would not. The *Town-Ho* encounters Moby Dick before Steelkilt can murder Radney, though, and, in the process of trying to harpoon the whale, Radney falls out of the boat. Moby Dick snatches him in his jaws. Ishmael's Peruvian listeners have a hard time believing the story, but he swears on a Bible that he is telling the truth and claims to have met and spoken with Steelkilt.

ANALYSIS: CHAPTERS 48–54
The appearance of Fedallah and his men changes the dynamic aboard the *Pequod.* Fedallah is an anomaly even in the culturally diverse whaling industry, and Ishmael describes him as a "muffled mystery to the last." Early in the novel, when Ishmael witnesses

Fedallah and the others slipping aboard the ship, and Elijah ominously alludes to them, it seems as if the *Pequod* has been boarded by ghosts or devils. Now Ishmael realizes that they are quite real, although they remain mysterious because of their aloofness and their connection to Ahab. Throughout the narrative, the reader finds it difficult to extricate the real from the supernatural, in part because Ahab exploits mystery and superstition for his own ends.

The concept of fate, in particular, serves Ahab's purposes, as he manipulates the crew into accepting that the hunt for the White Whale is their destiny. Fatalism, the belief in the inevitability of fate, is a perverse comfort to the sailors, enabling them to set aside their fears during times of danger since they believe that what will happen to them has already been determined by an external force. However, this supposed comfort doesn't stop the crew from looking for signs of their fate. The phantom spout, the fish that turn away from the *Pequod* to follow the *Albatross,* and the death of Radney in "The Town-Ho's Story" all foreshadow a catastrophic end to the *Pequod*'s quest. For Ishmael, acknowledging these signs and coming to terms with the extraordinary dangers of whaling brings a sense of relief. His belief in a predetermined fate lets him appreciate the present, and he comes to consider each new day as a gift.

Ahab, unlike his crew, views fate not as an externally determined destiny but as a way to justify his own perverse actions. He uses the idea of fate to motivate his crew and actively tries to determine his own "fate." Moby Dick will not find Ahab; rather, Ahab must seek Moby Dick out. For Ahab, fate is a fiction that allows him to pursue his vengeance: most of what he calls fate is the result of deliberately planned action.

The two "gams" in this section of the book are the first in a series of inset stories that come out of encounters with other ships. The gams highlight Ahab's unhealthy obsession by reminding the reader that men other than Ahab have encountered Moby Dick without reacting so irrationally to the experience. Gams are part of the normal social order of the seafaring world, and Ahab's unwillingness to participate in them unless he can use them to glean information relevant to his quest accentuates his eccentricity. The narrative uses gams to build a more complete picture of the maritime community: stories are traded, legends grow, and the social codes of the sailors are put on display.

CHAPTERS 55–65

CHAPTER 55: OF THE MONSTROUS PICTURES OF WHALES

Ishmael considers well-known graphic depictions of whales. To a whaleman who has actually seen whales, most historical, mythological, and scientific sources are blatantly inaccurate. As a result, says Ishmael, "you must needs conclude that the great Leviathan is that one creature in the world which must remain unpainted to the last." The only solution that Ishmael sees for one who seeks to know what a whale looks like is an actual encounter with the creature. In the ocean, only portions of a whale are visible at any one time, the majority of the animal being underwater. Only dead whales are visible in their near-entirety, and those are to the living animal what a wrecked ship is to one afloat. He warns the reader not to "be too fastidious in your curiosity" about the whale, since such curiosity is unlikely to be satisfied.

CHAPTER 56: OF THE LESS ERRONEOUS PICTURES OF
WHALES, AND THE TRUE PICTURES OF WHALING SCENES

Ishmael then tries to find some acceptable depictions of whales. To his mind, the only pictures that come close are two large French engravings that show the sperm and right whales in action. He wonders why the French have been best able to capture whales and whaling in art, because France is not a whaling nation.

CHAPTER 57: OF WHALES IN PAINT; IN TEETH; IN WOOD;
IN SHEET-IRON; IN STONE; IN MOUNTAINS; IN STARS

Ishmael considers versions of whales crafted by whalers, including specimens carved in ivory, wood, and metal. Those with an interest in the creature can see whales everywhere, including in geological forms and in the starry sky.

CHAPTER 58: BRIT

Brit is a minute yellow substance upon which the right whale feeds. Ishmael moves from a discussion of feeding whales to a generalized comparison between the land and the sea. In the sea, there are hidden horrors and continuous danger, while on land, all is visible and therefore manageable. He applies this assessment to the human soul, which he believes contains a small island of "peace and joy" surrounded by an ocean of horrors.

CHAPTER 59: SQUID

As the *Pequod* sails toward Java, Daggoo thinks that he sights Moby Dick. The boats are lowered and the animal pursued. It is a false alarm, however, as it is only a giant squid, which is taken as a bad omen. Ishmael notes that the squid is conjectured to be the sperm whale's food, but that the sperm whale feeds and lives largely out of sight beneath the sea's surface.

CHAPTER 60: THE LINE

In preparation for a later scene, says Ishmael, he will describe the whale-line. Made of hemp, this rope is connected to the harpoon at one end and dangles free at the other so that it can be tied to other boats' lines. Because it is laid out throughout the boat and whizzes out when a whale is darted, it is dangerous for the men of the harpoon crews. All men, according to Ishmael, live with metaphorical whale-lines around their necks, and it is only when a catastrophe occurs that they realize the constant perils of life.

CHAPTER 61: STUBB KILLS A WHALE

Queequeg views the squid as a good omen, indicating the presence of a sperm whale nearby. The crew soon sights a spouting sperm whale, which Stubb and Tashtego succeed in killing.

CHAPTER 62: THE DART

Ishmael gives a quick account of the harpooning of a whale. He argues that the system presently in use is inefficient, as the harpooner is forced to row strenuously before harpooning the whale and is thus breathing too hard to aim properly.

CHAPTER 63: THE CROTCH

The crotch is a wooden support for a harpoon. Ishmael quickly digresses from describing the crotch to consider the loose harpoons that pose a threat to the boats. Each line has two harpoons attached to it. Ideally, both would be thrown and stuck into the whale. More commonly, however, the whale dives after the first strike and the second harpoon must be thrown overboard to prevent injury to those in the boat. Dangling loose in the water, the second harpoon still poses a great danger to the boats.

CHAPTER 64: STUBB'S SUPPER

Most whalemen do not enjoy whale meat; Stubb, however, wants to dine on a steak from his whale. While he devours his steak, sharks dine on the carcass of the whale, which has been tied fast to the ship.

Stubb calls on the black cook, Fleece, to make his supper; he also demands that the cook order the sharks to stop eating the whale flesh. The cook delivers a sermon to the sharks, telling them that they ought to be more civilized. Stubb then proceeds to torment the cook, who likens Stubb to a shark.

CHAPTER 65: THE WHALE AS A DISH
Ishmael offers a culinary history of the whale. He remarks that no one except for Stubb and the Eskimos still eat it. Deterrents include the exceedingly rich quality of the meat and its prodigious quantities. Furthermore, it seems wrong to eat whale because, though hunting the whale makes the meat a "noble dish," one has to eat the meat by the light of a lamp that burns the whale's oil. But, Ishmael ponders, perhaps this adding of insult to injury isn't so rare: his readers probably eat beef with a knife made from the bone of oxen and pick their teeth after eating goose with a goose feather.

ANALYSIS: CHAPTERS 55–65
The chapters that survey visual depictions of whales demonstrate the cultural ubiquity of whales while simultaneously questioning the accuracy of pictures, and perhaps all representations, in general. Ishmael questions whether it is possible to create an object that conveys the reality and the spirit of the whale and its hunters. In doing so, he may implicitly suggest that his own picture of the whale—his narrative—will be inadequate. Alternatively, he may mean to imply the superiority of a picture in words to a graphic representation. The few engravings and paintings that Ishmael praises seem to be effective because they offer dramatic but not necessarily realistic scenes and convey some of the terror involved in a close encounter with a whale, which can also be said of Ishmael's narrative.

The sea, which offers only its surface for interpretation while hiding unknown events in its depths, is a perfect model of human perception. As Ishmael notes in Chapter 58 with his metaphor for the human soul, even when we examine ourselves, we see only surfaces and quick glimpses of hidden truths. Ishmael finds this limitation to human perception strangely liberating. Unaware of what lies beneath these surfaces, he is free to interpret the world as he sees fit. His narration in these chapters tends to begin with a discussion of something concrete like brit or the giant squid before veering into philosophical speculation about concepts like the human soul and the mysteries of the ocean.

Ishmael also offers the first of many digressions about whaling equipment and technique in these chapters. After describing the successful hunt of a whale, Ishmael goes back to talk about the crotch where a whale dart rests. His explanations about equipment and history give the novel a realistic and precise feel. This use of detail acts as a bulwark against the perceptual and philosophical uncertainty that threatens Ishmael's narrative. As a result, the novel at times reads more like a documentary than a work of fiction.

These chapters also include comic relief, in the person of the cook Fleece (whose name likely reflects the nineteenth-century American description of black people's hair as "woolly"). The cook's sermon to the sharks contrasts with Father Mapple's sermon in Chapter 9. Whereas Mapple delivers a lofty theological sermon full of metaphor and high ideals, Fleece addresses the sharks as "fellow-critters" and makes a series of startling points about equality, social justice, and the importance of distributing resources equally. Though it is supposed to be funny, his sermon resonates with Ishmael's mention of sharks following slave ships for a taste of their human cargo and with Stubb's mistreatment of the black Fleece. Fleece instances the undercurrent of racism and abuse within the supposedly meritocratic order aboard the *Pequod*.

CHAPTERS 66–73

CHAPTER 66: THE SHARK MASSACRE

The crew lashes the sperm whale they have caught to the side of the ship to be dealt with in daylight. But the men are forced to poke with spades or kill the numerous sharks that attempt to devour the whale carcass. Ishmael warns that it is unwise "to meddle with the corpses and ghosts of these creatures": Queequeg nearly has his hand cut off by the sharp teeth of one dead shark hoisted onto the ship for its skin.

CHAPTER 67: CUTTING IN

The gory business of "cutting-in," or processing the whale, commences. The cutting-in involves inserting a hook in the whale's blubber and peeling the blubber off as one might peel off an orange rind in one strip.

CHAPTER 68: THE BLANKET

As he describes the whale's blubber, Ishmael argues that this strip of flesh is actually the whale's skin. A thin and cellophane-like layer may be observed outside of the blubber, but this layer is only the skin of the skin. Ishmael admires the whale for its "thick walls," which allow it to live without being affected by its environment.

CHAPTER 69: THE FUNERAL

After the cutting-in, the whale is released for its "funeral," in which the "mourners" are vultures and sharks. The frightful white carcass floats away, and a "vengeful ghost" hovers over it, deterring other ships from going near it. Frequently, floating whale corpses are mistaken for rocks and shoals and thus entered on mariners' charts, causing future whalers to avoid the area. The whale thus continues to inspire terror even in death.

CHAPTER 70: THE SPHYNX

Ishmael describes the "scientific anatomical feat" of the whale's beheading, which occurs before the carcass is released; the head holds the valuable spermaceti, from which the finest oil comes. While the crew takes a break for a meal, Ahab talks to the whale's head hanging at the ship's side, asking it to tell him of the horrors that it has seen.

CHAPTER 71: THE JEROBOAM'S STORY

While Ahab converses with the whale, the *Jeroboam,* another whaling ship, sails into sight. An epidemic has broken out aboard her, so her captain doesn't board the *Pequod* but brings a small boat alongside for a talk with Ahab. Stubb recognizes one of the men at the oars of the boat as a man about whom he has heard from the crew of the *Town-Ho* during the last gam. This man, who had been a prophet among the Shakers in New York, proclaimed himself the archangel Gabriel on the ship, ordered the captain to jump overboard, and mesmerized the crew. The *Jeroboam*'s skipper, Captain Mayhew, wanted to get rid of Gabriel at the next port, but the crew threatened to desert if he was put ashore.

The sailors aboard the *Pequod* now see this very Gabriel in front of them. As Captain Mayhew tells Ahab a story about the White Whale, Gabriel interrupts continually. According to Mayhew, he and his men first heard about the existence of Moby Dick when they were speaking to another ship. Gabriel then warned against killing it, calling it "the Shaker God incarnated." They ran into Moby Dick a year later, and the ship's leaders decided to hunt it. As a mate stood in the ship to throw his lance, the whale flipped the mate into the air and tossed him into the sea. No one was harmed except for the mate, who drowned.

Gabriel had watched this episode from the masthead. The apparent fulfillment of his prophecy has led the crew to become his disciples.

When Ahab confirms that he still intends to hunt the White Whale, Gabriel points to him, saying, "Think, think of the blasphemer—dead, and down there!—beware of the blasphemer's end!" Ahab realizes that the *Pequod* is carrying a letter for the dead mate and tries to hand it over to Captain Mayhew on the end of a cutting-spade pole. Gabriel manages to grab it, impales it on the boat-knife, and sends it back to Ahab's feet as the *Jeroboam*'s boat pulls away.

CHAPTER 72: THE MONKEY-ROPE

Ishmael backtracks to explain how Queequeg initially inserts the blubber hook into the whale for the cutting-in. Ishmael, as Queequeg's bowsman, ties the monkey-rope around his own waist, "wedding" himself to Queequeg, who is on the whale's floating body trying to attach the hook. (In a footnote, we learn that only on the *Pequod* were the monkey and this holder actually tied together, an improvement introduced by Stubb, who found that it increases the reliability of the holder.) While Ishmael holds Queequeg, Tashtego and Daggoo brandish their whale-spades to keep the sharks away. When Dough-Boy, the steward, offers Queequeg some tepid ginger and water, the mates frown at the influence of pesky Temperance activists and make the steward bring him alcohol. The remainder of the ginger, a gift from "Aunt Charity," a Nantucket matron, is thrown overboard.

CHAPTER 73: STUBB AND FLASK KILL A RIGHT WHALE; AND THEN HAVE A TALK OVER HIM

The *Pequod* spots a right whale. After killing the whale, Stubb asks Flask what Ahab might want with this "lump of foul lard" (right whales were far less valuable than sperm whales). Flask responds that Fedallah says that a whaler with a sperm whale's head on her starboard side and a right whale's head on her larboard will never capsize afterward. They then both confess that they don't like Fedallah and think of him as "the devil in disguise." The right whale's head is lifted onto the opposite side of the boat from the sperm whale's head, and, in fact, the *Pequod* settles into balance. As Ishmael observes, however, the ship would float even better with neither head there. He observes Fedallah standing in Ahab's shadow and notes that Fedallah's shadow "seem[s] to blend with, and lengthen Ahab's."

ANALYSIS: CHAPTERS 66–73

This series of chapters juxtaposes the practical matters of whaling with a series of perceptual problems. The sharks that swarm around the boat seem to possess malevolent agency even after they are killed. Whale carcasses find their way into ships' logs as rocks or shoals, giving rise to long-lasting errors. Ishmael argues that the whale's blubber is its skin, but his argument suggests that any such classification of the whale's parts must be arbitrary. Such difficulties suggest that mistakes and misreadings cannot be avoided, and that comparison and approximation are the only means by which things can be described.

Instead of anthropomorphizing the whale—that is, assigning it human characteristics—Ishmael takes features of the whale and presents them as potential models for human life. He admires and envies the whale's blubber, which insulates the whale and enables it to withstand its environment, as evidenced by his cry of "Oh, man! admire and model thyself after the whale!" For Ishmael, however, the human acquiring of such an attribute has metaphorical significance: the idea of "remain[ing] warm among ice" hearkens back to the image, in Chapter 58, of the soul's small island of "peace and joy" amid terrorizing oceans. With its "rare virtue of a strong individual vitality," then, the whale, unlike man, according to Ishmael, exists in a sort of bliss of perfection, self-possession, and independence.

These chapters return to the topic of male bonding and homoeroticism explored in the early stages of the relationship between Queequeg and Ishmael. The monkey rope—"an elongated Siamese ligature"—connects the two men as if they were twins. They are joined in a "wedding" once again and, "should poor Queequeg sink to rise no more, then both usage and honor demand . . . that instead of cutting the cord, it should drag [Ishmael] down in his wake." This new bond makes the "till death do us part" clause of the Christian marriage ceremony literal: only death can sever the tie that binds Ishmael to Queequeg at this moment. As they depend on one another for their very lives, the bonds between the two are stronger than the relationship they had back on land. These men know they can trust one another because that trust is tested on a daily basis. This all-male world is more egalitarian, more open, and even more loving than the heterosexual world back home. By using the vocabulary of love and marriage—the primary relationships in our society—to describe the bonds between these men, Melville suggests that these shipboard pairings are models of ideal partnership.

The encounter with the *Jeroboam* is one of the most important of the series of visits that the *Pequod* entertains from other ships. The introduction of a group of outsiders provides perspective on the actions of Ahab and his crew. The appearance of the crazed prophet

Gabriel invites the reader to compare Gabriel's mental state to that of Ahab and Fedallah: each of these characters claims to possess prophetic or occult knowledge, but each of them may be crazy.

CHAPTERS 74–81

CHAPTER 74: THE SPERM WHALE'S HEAD — CONTRASTED VIEW

The two whale heads hanging from the *Pequod* provide an opportunity for Ishmael to give a lesson on "practical cetology." The sperm whale has a great well of sperm, ivory teeth, a long lower jaw, and one external spout hole. Ishmael describes the sperm whale as having "more character" than the right whale, as well as a "pervading dignity" based on the "mathematical symmetry" of its head. He wonders at the whale's small eyes, which are placed on opposite sides of its head, affording the whale a strange visual perspective. He notes also that the external portion of the whale's ear is tiny, comprised of only a small pinhole.

CHAPTER 75: THE RIGHT WHALE'S HEAD — CONTRASTED VIEW

The right whale, on the other hand, Ishmael explains, has bones in its mouth shaped like Venetian blinds, a huge lower lip, a tongue, and two external spout holes. He likens the right whale to a Stoic and the sperm whale to a "Platonian."

CHAPTER 76: THE BATTERING-RAM

Ishmael then points out that the blunt, large, wall-like part of the sperm whale's head seems to be just a "wad." In actuality, inside the thin, sturdy casing is a "mass of tremendous life." Ishmael notes that the whale's head, like many other things in nature, derives its strength from its flexibility and ability to be compressed and change shape.

CHAPTER 77: THE GREAT HEIDELBURGH TUN

Ishmael continues his survey by noting that the upper part of a whale's head has two subdivisions: the case and the junk. He compares the case to the "Great Heidelburgh Tun," a famous German wine vessel of enormous capacity. The case—which contains a reservoir of highly prized spermaceti, a valuable waxlike substance found in the oil—is carefully tapped once the whale's head has been suspended out of the water. The junk also contains oil, but this oil is trapped in a honeycomb of tough fibers.

CHAPTER 78: CISTERN AND BUCKETS
Ishmael describes Tashtego's tapping of the case. The sperm that it contains is lifted from the whale's head, which still dangles alongside the ship, to the deck by a relay of buckets. In tapping this whale, Tashtego accidentally falls into the case, which is at least twenty feet deep. In a panic, Daggoo clears the tangled lines and tries to get a line inside the head to Tashtego, but the tackle holding the head aloft breaks, and the great mass falls into the ocean. Queequeg dives in and manages to save Tashtego by cutting into the slowly sinking head and "delivering" Tashtego as a doctor would a baby.

CHAPTER 79: THE PRAIRIE
Ishmael applies the nineteenth-century arts of physiognomy (the art of judging human character from facial features) and phrenology (the study of the shape of the skull, based on the belief that it reveals character and mental capacity) to the whale. He considers the whale's features and, by means of physiognomic and phrenological analysis, concludes that the sperm whale's large, clear brow gives it the dignity of a god and that its "pyramidical silence" demonstrates its genius. But Ishmael then abandons this line of analysis, saying that he isn't a professional, and dares the reader to decipher the "hieroglyphics" of the sperm whale's brow.

CHAPTER 80: THE NUT
Ishmael then turns to the whale's skull, calling the whale's brow "false" because there really isn't much in the skull besides the sperm—its brain is only about ten inches across and is hidden behind some twenty feet of forehead. Ishmael then says that he would rather feel a man's spine than his skull to try to know him. If creatures were judged by their spines rather than their brains, he argues, people would discount the smallness of the whale's brain and admire the magnitude of his spinal cord. He believes that the whale's hump signifies its indomitable spirit.

CHAPTER 81: THE PEQUOD MEETS THE VIRGIN
The *Jungfrau* (Virgin) is out of oil, as she has had no success in catching whales. Her captain boards the *Pequod* to beg for some. Ahab asks about the White Whale, but the *Jungfrau* has no information. Almost immediately after the captain of the *Jungfrau* steps off the *Pequod*'s deck, whales are sighted, and the captain goes after them desperately. The *Pequod* also gives chase and succeeds in harpooning a slower whale before the Germans can catch it. The whale is

old, blind, and covered with growths, and in its flesh the crew finds an ancient-looking stone harpoon point. After bringing the carcass alongside the ship, the crew discovers that the whale is sinking and dragging the ship down with it. Ishmael then notes that it is impossible to predict which whales will sink. The inexperienced crew of the *Jungfrau* then starts chasing a finback, a whale that to the unskilled observer resembles a sperm whale but is too fast a swimmer to be caught.

ANALYSIS: CHAPTERS 74–81

Though he attempts simply to describe the whale heads accurately, Ishmael is soon tempted into making imaginative comparisons between the heads and schools of classical philosophy (Stoic and "Platonian.") Additionally, phrenology and physiognomy, popular in the nineteenth century, are only pseudoscientific. Physiognomy was widely used in the study of criminal behavior and as a justification of discrimination against the poor and against certain racial groups. Likewise, phrenology was also used to justify racial inequality, and gave rise to the judgmental terms "highbrow" and "lowbrow." As such, these disciplines, which developed out of subjective and therefore biased principles, hardly constitute rational inquiry.

As he considers the whale, Ishmael continuously probes deeper. From the outer surface of the skin, he moves in to the blubber; from the outer skull, he moves in to the "nut" or brain. This inward progression suggests an attempt to get at the heart, or inner meaning, of things and recalls Ahab's statement that he must "strike through the mask," or outward appearance. Ishmael explicitly connects this mode of investigation to reading. Phrenology and physiognomy, he says, are simply alternate forms of reading; instead of reading books, one reads skulls and faces. In saying "I but put that brow before you. Read it if you can," Ishmael offers a challenge to his reader to make sense of the bumps and curves of *Moby-Dick*. The connection between reading and these pseudosciences is a warning, though, that reading is subject to the reader's own biases. The multiplicity of readings of the whale's head, each based on a different discipline or a different set of principles, is a reminder that any single approach is insufficient and that an interdisciplinary approach may yield the most fruitful interpretations.

The rescue of Tashtego from the sinking whale's head is one of the most unusual moments of the novel, both in terms of the action itself and the language used to describe it. Ishmael describes the process as a rebirth, an exercise in "obstetrics." This depiction recalls Ishmael's earlier notion that whalers are men already dead. Tashtego, like the biblical Lazarus, has died and been reborn, and any extra days of his life are a gift. His rebirth also parodies religious images of resurrection. Tashtego is "delivered" from death not by Christ but by a fellow man—a non-Christian at that. Finally, Ishmael's obstetrics comparison points to a heightened level of linguistic play that characterizes much of the rest of the novel. As the men of the *Pequod* work together, their experience comes to encompass metaphorically all aspects of life, from birth to sexual maturation to death. Ishmael's language reflects this broad experience and mediates between the crude speech of real sailors, the aesthetic demands of the novel, and the genteel sensibilities of Melville's nineteenth-century reader.

Juxtaposed as it is with Tashtego's rescue, the encounter with the *Jungfrau* is subtly humorous, as the "virgin" ship would have no need for an obstetrician. The *Jungfrau* and the *Pequod* can be read, respectively, as innocence and experience. The naive *Jungfrau* chases illusions and engages in frivolous activities, while the more worldly *Pequod* austerely chases death. The whale for which the *Pequod* competes against the *Jungfrau* provides one of the most dramatic incidents of foreshadowing in the narrative so far. As if out of vengeance for its death, the whale seems to intentionally sink the *Pequod*. Given the description of the dying whale that Ishmael has just offered, in which he details the creature's humanlike suffering, this seeming vengeance is not at all surprising—the natural world is as vengeful as Ahab.

CHAPTERS 82–92

CHAPTER 82: THE HONOR AND GLORY OF WHALING
Ishmael considers the heroic history of whaling. He draws from Greek mythology, popular British legend, the Judeo-Christian Bible, and Hindu mythology: Perseus, St. George, Hercules, Jonah, and Vishnu (whose name Melville spells "Vishnoo") can all be considered whalemen based on the stories told about their exploits.

CHAPTER 83: JONAH HISTORICALLY REGARDED
Ishmael examines the Jonah story—which has shadowed the novel ever since the "Extracts" and Father Mapple's sermon in New Bedford—through the eyes of an old Sag Harbor whaleman who questions the tale based on his personal experience. Sag Harbor, as

Ishmael calls him, doesn't believe that a whale of the kind described in the Bible could swallow a man, and he thinks that a whale's gastric juices would not permit a man to survive in the whale's stomach. Ishmael details various theologians' arcane responses to such practical questions.

CHAPTER 84: PITCHPOLING
Ishmael describes the process of oiling a harpoon boat's underside to increase speed. He reports that Queequeg performs this task carefully, seemingly with an awareness that the *Pequod* will encounter whales later that day. Stubb harpoons a fast and tireless whale. In order to capture it, he must "pitchpole" it by throwing a long lance from the jerking boat to secure the running whale. Stubb's lance strikes home, and the whale spouts blood.

CHAPTER 85: THE FOUNTAIN
With an attempt at scientific precision, Ishmael discusses how whales spout. He cannot define exactly what the spout is, so he has to put forward a hypothesis: the spout is nothing but mist, like the "semi-visible steam" emitted from the head of such ponderous beings as Plato, Pyrrho, the Devil, Jupiter, Dante, and even himself.

CHAPTER 86: THE TAIL
Ishmael then considers the opposite end of the animal, celebrating the whale's most famous part: its tail. He admires its combination of power and grace, and muses that it represents the whale's attempts to reach to heaven—the tail is often seen protruding toward the skies. Whether this positioning is viewed as an act of angelic adoration or demoniac defiance (like the shaking of a fist) on the whale's part depends on the mood of the spectator. Ishmael notes that the tail is the sperm whale's most frequent means of inflicting injury upon men.

CHAPTER 87: THE GRAND ARMADA
When the *Pequod* sails through the straits of Sunda (near Indonesia) without pulling into any port, Ishmael takes the opportunity to discuss the isolation and self-containment of a whaling ship. While in the straits, the *Pequod* encounters a great herd of sperm whales swimming in a circle (the "Grand Armada"), but, as the ship chases the whales, it is itself pursued by Malay pirates. The *Pequod* escapes the pirates and launches boats after the whales, somehow ending up inside their circle, a placid lake. One harpooned whale flounders in pain, causing panic among the whole herd. The boats in the middle are in danger but manage to escape the chaos. They "drugg" the

whales by attaching lines with large blocks of wood attached, which provide resistance and tire the swimming whales. The whalemen also try to "waif" the whales, marking them with pennoned poles as the *Pequod*'s, to be taken later. They succeed in capturing only one whale.

CHAPTER 88: SCHOOLS AND SCHOOLMASTERS

Ishmael takes a moment to explain some whaling terms, beginning with "schools" of whales. Schools are typically composed of one male—the "schoolmaster" or "lord"—and numerous females, the "harem." When whalers find a school, they hunt only the females and calves, as the males are too large and dangerous. As the male whales age, they leave their harems behind and become solitary, ill-tempered wanderers. The all-male schools are like a "mob of young collegians." The major difference between the males and the females, according to Ishmael, is that males abandon injured comrades while females do not, even risking their own lives to aid and comfort a friend.

CHAPTER 89: FAST-FISH AND LOOSE-FISH

Ishmael takes some time to explain his reference to "waifs" in Chapter 87. He goes on to talk about whaling codes past and present, which say that a "Fast-Fish" belongs to the party fast to it (the party that has laid claim to it) and a "Loose-Fish" is fair game for anybody who can catch it. A fish is "fast" when it is physically connected to the party after it or when it bears a waif, or marker. Lawyerlike, Ishmael cites precedents and stories to show how difficult it is to maintain rules, especially when they admit so much ambiguity. Metaphorically, everything in the world can be conceptualized according to the code that judges possession to be the sole legal criterion of ownership. Even entire nations, Ishmael observes, can be classified as "Fast-Fish" or "Loose-Fish" and colonized accordingly by more powerful nations.

CHAPTER 90: HEADS OR TAILS

Ishmael elaborates upon the strange fishing laws of England, which state that any whale or sturgeon captured on its coast is "fast" and belongs to England. The head must be given to the king and the tail to the queen, leaving nothing for the hunter. Ishmael tells the story of some poor whalemen who lost all profits from their hard-earned whale to a wealthy duke.

Chapter 91: The Pequod Meets the Rose-Bud

The *Pequod* encounters a French ship, the *Bouton de Rose* (Rose-Button or Rose-Bud), from which a terrible stench arises. This ship has two whales alongside: one "blasted whale" (a whale that died unmolested on the sea) that is going to have nothing useful in it and one whale that died from indigestion. Stubb asks a sailor aboard the *Rose-Bud* if they have any news of Moby Dick. The man answers that they have never heard of the White Whale. Crafty Stubb asks why the man is trying to get oil out of these whales when clearly there is none in either. The sailor replies that his captain, on his first trip, will not believe the sailor's own statements that the whales are worthless. Stubb goes aboard to tell the captain that the whales are worthless, although he knows something that the other sailor doesn't: the second whale might contain ambergris, a valuable substance found in the intestines of sick whales. Stubb gets the sailor to help him trick the French captain into thinking that the "blasted" whales pose a threat of infection to the crew. The captain dumps the whales and Stubb, pretending to be helpful, has the *Pequod*'s boats tow the second whale away. As soon as the *Rose-Bud* leaves, Stubb ties up to the second whale and finds the sweet-smelling ambergris inside it.

Chapter 92: Ambergris

Ishmael explains that ambergris, though it looks like mottled cheese and comes from the bowels of whales, is actually used for perfumes. He ponders the origin of the idea that whales smell bad. In the past, whaling vessels were unable to render blubber into oil at sea, and the rotting blubber created a powerful stench when they arrived in port. The rendered oil, however, is odorless and a natural cleanser. Ishmael notes that live whales, like beautiful women, actually smell pleasantly musky.

Analysis: Chapters 82–92

Chapters 82 and 83 explore ways in which texts are misread and distorted. The story of Jonah is the subject of Father Mapple's sermon in Chapter 9, and Mapple himself might be regarded as the ideal reader. His imagination seizes upon what is important in a story without getting bogged down in extraneous details. Sag Harbor, in contrast, is so lost in technical objections that he misses the symbolic meaning of the Jonah story. The theologians whom Ishmael cites to counter Sag Harbor seem equally ludicrous, since they too ignore the story's underlying message, spinning ever more contorted explanations to maintain that every detail of the story is true. In Chapter 82, Ishmael himself is guilty of similar distortions when he ignores the totality of the careers of Hercules, St. George, and others to argue that they are whalemen.

The imagery in this section stresses ambiguity. Death and birth are connected as the blood of the panicked, hurt whales mingles with the milk that the calves are drinking when the "Grand Armada" of whales is attacked. When the *Pequod* chases the whales, it is in turn chased by pirates, illustrating that ocean life involves a repeating cycle of events; we thus come to understand the story of the *Pequod* from a larger, more philosophical perspective. This interchangeability of parts also suggests some equivalence between the men on the *Pequod* and the whales. Indeed, particularly in the chapter on "Schools and Schoolmasters," Ishmael gives the whale a range of human qualities. This anthropomorphizing (giving human attributes to nonhuman entities) suggests that hunting whales is exploitative and even murderous. Critics have suggested that *Moby-Dick* can be read as an analogue to other forms of exploitation by white men, such as slavery, colonialism, and territorial expansion.

CHAPTERS 93–101

CHAPTER 93: THE CASTAWAY
Pip, the *Pequod*'s cabin boy, is drafted to be a replacement oarsman in Stubb's harpoon boat. Having performed passably the first time out, Pip goes out in the harpoon boat a second time. This time, however, he jumps from the boat in fear when the whale raps the bottom of the boat beneath his seat. Pip's boatmates become angry when they have to cut the whale loose in order to save Pip after he gets tangled in the lines. Stubb tells him never to jump out of the boat again, threatening not to pick him up next time. But Pip does jump again, and to teach him a lesson, Stubb leaves him alone in the middle of the sea's "heartless immensity." This experience drives him mad, at least insofar as his shipmates can observe. Ishmael, on the other hand, declares that the experience endows Pip with divine wisdom.

CHAPTER 94: A SQUEEZE OF THE HAND
Because the spermaceti taken from a whale's head quickly cools into lumps, the sailors have to squeeze it back into liquid. Ishmael is carried away with enthusiasm for the "sweet and unctuous" sperm. He

squeezes all morning long, sentimentally describing his physical contact with the other sailors, whose hands he unintentionally gropes in the vat of sperm. He also describes some of the other tissues of the whale from which oil is derived. He gives a brief glimpse into the ship's "blubber-room," where the blubber is cut into sections and prepared for rendering. The blubber-room is a dark and dangerous place: the blubber-men frequently lose toes to the sharp spades used to cut the blubber.

CHAPTER 95: THE CASSOCK

Ishmael describes the other parts of the whale, including the penis, euphemistically named the "cassock." He blasphemously likens the whale's organ to the dress of clergymen because it has some pagan mysticism attached to it. It also serves a practical purpose on the ship: the mincer wears the black "pelt" of skin from the penis to protect himself while he slices the pieces of blubber for the pots.

CHAPTER 96: THE TRY-WORKS

[E]ven in his lowest swoop the mountain eagle is still higher than other birds upon the plain, even though they soar.

(See QUOTATIONS, *p. 76)*

Ishmael attempts to explain the try-works, a set of pots and furnaces that boil the blubber and derive all the oil from it. He associates the try-works with darkness and a sense of exotic evil: it has "an unspeakable, wild, Hindoo odor about it, such as may lurk in the vicinity of funereal pyres." Furthermore, the pagan harpooners tend it. Ishmael comments that the hellish red fires of the try-works, combined with the black sea and the dark night, so disorient him that he loses his sense of himself at the tiller. Everything becomes "inverted," he says, and suddenly there is "no compass before me to steer by."

CHAPTER 97: THE LAMP

Whalemen are always in the light, Ishmael explains, because their job is to collect oil from the seas. These men have free access to the oil, and each keeps a collection of lamps in his bunk. The interior of the ship is illuminated like a temple.

CHAPTER 98: STOWING DOWN AND CLEARING UP

Ishmael completes his description of how whale oil is processed. The oil is put in casks and the ship is cleaned. Here he dismisses another myth about whaling, asserting that whalers are *not* inherently dirty. Sperm whale oil, in fact, is a fine cleaning agent. Ishmael must admit, however, that whalers are clean for barely a day when the next whale is sighted and the cycle begins again.

CHAPTER 99: THE DOUBLOON

Ishmael returns to his shipmates, describing the reactions of Ahab, Starbuck, Stubb, Flask, the Manxman (a sailor from the Isle of Man, off the coast of England), Queequeg, Fedallah, and Pip to the golden coin fixed on the mainmast. The doubloon features a picture of three mountain peaks, one topped by a flame, one by a tower, and one by a rooster. Above the mountains, the sky is divided into a segment of the zodiac, with the sun entering the constellation Libra. Ahab remarks that the round coin is like the world in that man can see himself in it. Starbuck interprets it as a Christian symbol. Stubb, who had thought of the coin only as money to be spent, looks deeper at the doubloon after seeing his two superiors gaze meaningfully at it. Consulting his almanac to identify the zodiacal symbols, Stubb reflects that such books supply only bare facts, whereas people supply the thoughts that make facts meaningful.

He proceeds to interpret the entire zodiac as an allegory for the life of man. Flask sees only the monetary value of the coin and cannot understand what all of the staring has been about. The Manxman concludes that the ship will encounter the White Whale in a month and a day, when the sun is in the section of the zodiac depicted on the coin. Queequeg compares the coin to a tattoo on his leg but says nothing, while Fedallah makes a sign of reverence to the coin, perhaps because he is a sun worshipper. Pip looks last and says, portentously, that the coin is the ship's "navel"—the thing at the center of the ship that holds it together.

CHAPTER 100: LEG AND ARM: THE PEQUOD, OF NANTUCKET, MEETS THE SAMUEL ENDERBY, OF LONDON

The *Pequod* meets the *Samuel Enderby,* a whaling ship from London with a jolly captain and crew. Ahab asks if the other crew has encountered Moby Dick. The captain, named Boomer, has, and he lacks an arm because of it. The two mutilated captains touch their false limbs in a toast. The account of Boomer's lost arm is gory, but Boomer doesn't dwell too much on the horrible details, choosing instead to talk about the hot rum toddies that he drank during his recovery. From the little that he says, the *Pequod* men gather that Boomer was injured by a loose harpoon dangling from a line

attached to Moby Dick. His arm was not severed but was ampu-
tated when the wound became gangrenous. The ship encountered the
White Whale again, but, having learned his lesson, Boomer didn't try to
hunt it a second time. Ahab insists on knowing which way the whale
went; the *Samuel Enderby*'s crew believes him crazy. Refusing the other
crew's hospitality, Ahab abruptly returns to his ship.

CHAPTER 101: THE DECANTER
Ishmael explains the significance of the name Samuel Enderby: this
man fitted the first English sperm whaling ship. Ishmael is careful to
point out that Americans had already been sperm-whaling for some
time when the English got into the industry. He then offers some of the
history behind the Enderby name before telling the story of the particular
whaler *Samuel Enderby*. This and other British ships are well known for
their hospitality, particularly in the way of alcoholic beverages.

ANALYSIS: CHAPTERS 93–101
The chapters in this section present a bewildering array of materials.
The section is framed by the stories of Pip and Captain Boomer, each
of whom undergoes a trauma at sea and responds to that trauma in
his own way. Boomer's acceptance of his mutilation provides a
sharp contrast to Ahab's furious thirst for vengeance. Indeed, the fellowship and good cheer represented by the *Samuel Enderby,* as well as
its crew's unwillingness to pursue a hopeless and fatal quest, suggest a
much more appealing way of going through life than the monomaniacal pursuit of a single goal represented by Ahab and the *Pequod.*

The chapters in which Ishmael describes the processing of the
whale's body contribute to the reader's factual understanding of the
ship's activities and purpose; more important, however, these activities provide the material upon which Ishmael exercises his imaginative and speculative faculties. His rhapsody about the pleasures of
kneading the sperm with his fellow sailors is particularly striking,
both for its obvious homoeroticism and for the remarkable conclusion that he draws from it. Life experience has gradually taught him
that human beings cannot make themselves happy by pursuing
vague or abstract goals, that they always have to shift their goals to
pursue something concrete: a spouse, the pleasures of bed, the comfort of the fireside, the beauty of the countryside. With this outlook,
Ishmael realizes that the pleasures of squeezing sperm with the other
sailors are as real and perfect as any happiness in life.

The doubloon chapter makes a number of startling points about how people interpret the world. Ahab asserts that whether they look at a symbol or the entire world, they see a reflection of themselves. His statements that the firm tower, fiery volcano, and courageous fowl are all Ahab is thus self-consciously ironic—he knows that he projects himself onto the symbol. But this realization does not lead Ahab to examine himself critically as he examines the design on the coin. Instead, Ahab seems to conclude that people are simply trapped, unable to see anything but themselves, and thus can never grow or change.

The other sailors' comments on the coin bear out Ahab's point. Starbuck sees the coin as an emblem of the world that he sees around him: a vale of death, in which God, represented by the sun, offers a beacon of hope but no certainty. Stubb insightfully points out that human imagination must supply much of the meaning of any symbol, and, on seeing the zodiac apparently for the first time, he constructs a dazzling interpretation of the zodiacal signs as representing the twelve stages of a person's life. The picture of human life that results is typical of Stubb's fatalistic yet comical outlook.

CHAPTERS 102–114

CHAPTER 102: A BOWER IN THE ARSACIDES

Ishmael tries to understand the whale by measuring its bones. In an effort to bolster his credibility in describing the whale, he tells of a visit to his friend Tranquo, king of Tranque (apparently a fictional place). In Tranque, a large sperm whale skeleton is used as a temple, with its skull as an altar. Although the priests protested, claiming that it is impossible to measure God, Ishmael took the whale's dimensions and had them tattooed on his right arm. He had the dimensions recorded in short form because he wished to save as much space on his body as possible for "a blank page for a poem [he] was then composing."

CHAPTER 103: MEASUREMENT OF THE WHALE'S SKELETON

Ishmael offers his findings, based on the skeleton of the whale that he measured in Tranque. He believes that the largest sperm whales are around ninety tons, and "would considerably outweigh the combined population of a whole village of one thousand one hundred inhabitants." He then gives detailed dimensions of all parts of the whale's skeleton. These bones, he cautions, give only a partial picture of the whale, since so much flesh is wrapped around them and they don't capture the essence of the living animal. He adds that a person cannot find a good representation of a whale in its entirety.

CHAPTER 104: THE FOSSIL WHALE

Ishmael admits that he is "manhandling" the whale in his description, but he says that he is doing the best that he knows how. He decides to look at the Fossil Whale from an "archaeological, fossiliferous, and antediluvian point of view." He states that it is impossible for him to exaggerate with the words that he uses to describe the whale because the whale itself is so grand. He establishes his credentials as a geologist and presents his findings. Once again, he is unsatisfied with the picture of the whale that he has created: "the skeleton of the whale furnishes but little clue to the shape of his fully invested body." This chapter gives a sense of the whale's age as a species and his pedigree, and allows Ishmael to meditate on time as a construct of man.

CHAPTER 105: DOES THE WHALE'S MAGNITUDE DIMINISH? — WILL HE PERISH?

In awe of his subject, Ishmael finally admits defeat in his attempts to capture the whale through description. Now he questions whether such a fabulous monster will remain on the earth and if, as reports have it, its size is diminishing over time. Based on the fact that man and other animals have actually gotten larger throughout history, Ishmael believes that it is not likely that the whale has diminished in size. As for the whale's continued survival, Ishmael says that though whales may not travel in herds anymore and though their haunts may have changed, they remain nonetheless. He believes that their survival owes to the new home base they have established at the poles, where man cannot penetrate. He also notes that other large mammals have been extensively hunted and that the whale population is likely not in danger because it has an enormous home environment and because many generations of whales are alive at the same time. In fact, whales are particularly likely to endure—if there is another Noah's flood, Ishmael remarks, whales will not drown.

CHAPTER 106: AHAB'S LEG

Ahab asks the carpenter to make him a new leg, as the one that he uses is not trustworthy. After hitting it heavily on the boat's wooden floor when he returned from the *Samuel Enderby,* Ahab feels that his leg won't continue to hold together. Indeed, just before the *Pequod* sailed from Nantucket, Ishmael relates, Ahab had been found lying on the ground with the whalebone leg twisted around and almost piercing his groin.

CHAPTER 107: THE CARPENTER

The carpenter, the do-it-all man on the ship, has to make Ahab a new prosthetic leg. The carpenter is an able man, but he views everything, even parts of the human body, as pieces of a machine.

CHAPTER 108: AHAB AND THE CARPENTER: THE DECK—FIRST NIGHT WATCH

In this playlike scene, Ahab approaches the carpenter to be fitted for his new leg. He abuses the carpenter and discourses on hell and the feeling of a ghost leg. When Ahab leaves, the carpenter muses on the captain's queerness.

CHAPTER 109: AHAB AND STARBUCK IN THE CABIN

Sailors discover that the oil casks in the hold are leaking. Starbuck informs Ahab and suggests that they stop to fix them, but Ahab refuses to stop, saying that he doesn't care about the owners or profit. Starbuck objects, and Ahab points a musket at him. Says Starbuck, "I ask thee not to beware of Starbuck; thou wouldst but laugh; but let Ahab beware of Ahab; beware of thyself, old man." After Starbuck departs, Ahab abruptly gives in and orders the casks repaired. Ishmael speculates that Ahab's decision was a "prudential policy" to avoid angering the crew.

CHAPTER 110: QUEEQUEG IN HIS COFFIN

While the repairs are being made to the casks, Queequeg falls ill. Thinking he is going to die, he orders a coffin made and fills it with his harpoon, his idol, and various other important possessions. He lies in it and closes the cover, and Pip dances around the coffin. Pip asks Queequeg to look for the former's old, sane self in paradise after he dies. Queequeg soon feels well again and emerges from his coffin. Ishmael attributes this recovery to Queequeg's "savage" nature—Queequeg claims that he has willed himself back to health. Queequeg uses the coffin as a chest for his belongings and sets about copying the tattoos on his body onto the lid of the coffin. The tattoos were done by a prophet among his people and are supposed to depict "a complete theory of the heavens and the earth, and a mystical treatise on the art of attaining truth."

CHAPTER 111: THE PACIFIC

Ishmael ponders the meditative, serene Pacific Ocean. The sea promotes dreaminess and seems like heaven to him. Ishmael considers Ahab, noting that no such calming thoughts stir the captain's brain.

CHAPTER 112: THE BLACKSMITH

Ishmael then describes the *Pequod*'s blacksmith, whose life on land disintegrated after he turned to drink. Echoing his own initial reasons for shipping aboard the *Pequod,* Ishmael explains that the sea beckons to brokenhearted men who long for death but cannot commit suicide.

CHAPTER 113: THE FORGE

Ahab asks the blacksmith to make a special harpoon with which to kill the White Whale. He gives the blacksmith the stubs of the nails of racehorse shoes, the toughest steel known, with which to make the weapon. Although Ahab gives the blacksmith directions, he soon takes over the crafting of the harpoon himself, hammering the steel on the anvil and tempering it with the blood of the three harpooners instead of water. The scene ends with Pip's laughter ringing through the ship.

CHAPTER 114: THE GILDER

The dreaminess of the sea masks its ferocity. Ishmael speaks of the sea as "gilt" because it looks golden in the sunset and is falsely calm. The soothing scene inspires Ahab, Starbuck, and Stubbs to address the sea philosophically, each in his characteristic way.

ANALYSIS: CHAPTERS 102–114

In the first four chapters in this section, Ishmael continues to search for a way to represent the whale in its totality. He also becomes more concerned with conceptualizing what he does as a writer and what gives his words authority. Just as the Tranque priests claim that God cannot be measured, Ishmael proves that the whale cannot be comprehended in its totality by means of an empirical description of its parts. However, such partial details are all that a writer has to work with.

Ishmael establishes his authority to write about the skeletons and fossil history of whales by recounting his trip to Tranque and his work as a stonemason and trench-digger. While these credentials are clearly ridiculous—Tranque is fictional, and a trench-digger cannot claim to be an expert on fossils—they point to his growing attention to the task of writing. In Chapter 85, Ishmael refers to the writer as a "profound being" who has little to say to the world but is "forced to stammer out something by way of getting a living." But in later chapters he seems unsure of his own profundity, focusing instead on experience as the source of narrative. He explains his own choice of tone and diction as expanding to fit his subject—the whale—which is both physically and symbolically enormous.

In Ishmael's narrative, tattoos combine writing and experience in unexpected ways. The measurements tattooed on his arm make Ishmael's body a living record of his experience. Moreover, he speaks of his plan to tattoo a much longer document on his body at some point in the future. Tattooing, as mentioned earlier, was seen in the nineteenth century as an irreversible mark of difference, testifying to an individual's separation from conventional white society. Ishmael's tattoos serve as a reminder that he has had experiences very different from those of a typical white man. Queequeg's tattoos also function as a record of experience and knowledge. They depict his culture's understanding of the universe and truth. Tradition and learning are passed on from person to person, and every person is a book, albeit in not quite so literal a fashion as Queequeg. Having no one from his home to whom he can pass on the knowledge inscribed on his body, Queequeg copies his tattoos onto his coffin, the symbol of his inevitable death. Appropriately, the coffin survives to the end of the novel, enabling the information carved on its lid to survive as well, just as the novel that Ishmael writes will survive his eventual death.

In these chapters, scenes of high drama alternate with scenes of tranquility and dreamlike peace. As earlier, some of these chapters are written as if they were scenes from a play. Dialogues, soliloquies, and asides are used with increasing frequency, which reminds the reader that Ahab is concocting his own drama and that the quest for Moby Dick is as artificial as a play. The alternation of dreamy contemplation with dramatic tension reflects the reality of whaling: the excitement of the hunt is tempered by long periods of watching and waiting.

CHAPTERS 115–125

CHAPTER 115: THE PEQUOD MEETS THE BACHELOR

The somber *Pequod,* still on the lookout for Moby Dick, encounters the *Bachelor,* a festive Nantucket whaler on its way home with a full cargo. The captain of the *Bachelor,* saying that he has heard stories of the White Whale but doesn't believe them, invites Ahab and the crew to join his party. Ahab declines, and the two ships go their separate ways as Ahab contemplates a vial of Nantucket sand that he has been carrying in his pocket.

CHAPTER 116: THE DYING WHALE

The next day, the *Pequod* kills several whales, and the way that one dying whale turns toward the sun inspires Ahab to speak to it in wondrous tones. He notes that the whale, like man, worships the sun's warmth. Ahab then hails the sea, calling its waves his "foster-brothers."

CHAPTER 117: THE WHALE WATCH

While keeping a night vigil over a whale that was too far away to take back to the ship immediately, Ahab hears from Fedallah the prophecy of his death. Before Ahab can die, he must see two hearses, one "not made by mortal hands" and one made of wood from America. Since it is unlikely that a hearse would be seen at sea, Ahab believes that he will not be killed on this voyage. Fedallah also tells him that he, Fedallah, will die before Ahab, and that only hemp can kill the captain. Ahab takes the latter prophecy to mean that he will be hanged, and again thinks his death unlikely to happen at sea.

CHAPTER 118: THE QUADRANT

Back on the ship, Ahab holds up a quadrant, an instrument that gauges the position of the sun, to determine the ship's latitude. Deciding that it doesn't give him the information that he wants, he tramples it underfoot. He orders the ship to change direction. Starbuck finds Ahab's ambitions petty and thinks that his behavior will end in mediocrity and failure. Stubb, on the other hand, respects Ahab for his willingness to "live in the game, and die in it!"

CHAPTER 119: THE CANDLES

The next day, the *Pequod* is caught in a typhoon, and one of the harpoon boats is destroyed. The weird weather makes white flames appear at the top of the three masts, but Ahab refuses to let the crew put up lightning rods to draw away the danger. While Ahab marvels at the ship's three masts lit up like three spermaceti candles, hailing them as good omens and signs of his own power, Starbuck sees them as a warning against continuing the quest for Moby Dick. When Starbuck sees Ahab's harpoon also flickering with fire, he interprets it as a sign that God opposes Ahab. Ahab, however, grasps the harpoon and says, in front of a frightened crew, that there is nothing to fear in the enterprise that binds them all together. He blows out the flame to "blow out the last fear."

Chapter 120: The Deck Towards the End of the First Night Watch

In the next chapter, Starbuck questions Ahab's judgment again, this time concerning the sails during the storm. Starbuck wants to take one of them down, but Ahab says that they should just lash it tighter. He complains that his first mate seems to think him incompetent.

Chapter 121: Midnight—the Forecastle Bulwarks

Stubb and Flask have their own conversation about the storm and Ahab's behavior. Stubb dominates the conversation and insists that this journey is no more dangerous than any other, even though it seems as if Ahab is putting them in extreme danger.

Chapter 122: Midnight Aloft—Thunder and Lightning

Suspended above the men on the main-top-sail yard, Tashtego thinks to himself that sailors care more about rum than about the storm.

Chapter 123: The Musket

When the storm finally dies down, Starbuck goes below to report to Ahab. On the way to the cabin, he sees a row of muskets, including the very one that Ahab had leveled at him earlier. Angry about Ahab's reckless and selfish behavior, he debates with himself about whether he ought to kill his captain. He decides that he cannot kill Ahab in his sleep and returns to the deck, asking Stubb to wake Ahab.

Chapter 124: The Needle

When Ahab is on deck the next day, he realizes that the storm has thrown off the compasses. He then pronounces himself "lord over the level loadstone yet" and makes his own needle. Here Ishmael notes that "[i]n this fiery eye of scorn and triumph, you then saw Ahab in all his fatal pride."

Chapter 125: The Log and Line

With all of the other orienting devices out of order, Ahab decides to pull out the seldom-used log and line, a device used to measure a ship's speed. Because of heat and moisture, the line breaks, and Ahab realizes that he now has none of his original navigational devices. He calls for Pip to help him, but Pip answers with nonsense. Ahab, touched by Pip's crazy speeches, says that his cabin will now be Pip's, because the boy touches his "inmost center."

ANALYSIS: CHAPTERS 115–125

Ishmael fades in and out of his own narration in these chapters, as Ahab's determination and control over the ship increase. Many of these chapters, in fact, are made up entirely of soliloquies and asides, for which it seems unlikely that Ishmael would have been an audience. The events that occur in these chapters also reflect Ahab's increasing power over the ship. First Ahab throws away the quadrant. He then refuses to put up the lightning rods, makes his own compass, and breaks the log and line. These devices are the only things that keep the *Pequod* on an objective, standard course. The loss of the ship's compass is probably most significant—its replacement with one of Ahab's own manufacture suggests that the *Pequod*'s path will now be dictated not by logic, skill, or convention but solely by Ahab's will.

Ahab has become so self-confident that he alters the prophecy delivered by Fedallah, his own private prophet, in order to make it conform to his own vision. For every part of Fedallah's prophecy, Ahab finds a reason that it will not apply to him. He assumes, for instance, that Fedallah's assertion that only hemp can cause Ahab's death means that he is to be hung. Ahab ignores the fact that he is on a ship hung with ropes, which are used in every aspect of sailing and whaling. Ishmael even frequently notes the sort of fatal accidents involving rope that can occur. Ahab's willful misreading of Fedallah's words demonstrates his hubris, or arrogant overconfidence.

Ahab acquires an unexpected double in the person of Pip. Pip and Ahab complement each other in many ways: Ahab is white, while Pip is black; Ahab is at the center of the intrigue, while Pip is marginal; Ahab is atop the shipboard hierarchy, while Pip is at the bottom; Ahab is old and wise, while Pip is young and knows nothing about whaling technique. Most important, however, Ahab seems to possess a modicum of sanity, while Pip seems to have crossed the line into insanity. Despite these differences, both see the world slightly aslant and feel alienated from the majority of the men on the ship. Their situation, as Pip explains it, creates between them a "man-rope; something that weak souls may hold by." Pip pulls at the deeply buried remnants of Ahab's humanity, and Ahab takes Pip almost as a son.

A crucial difference between Pip and Ahab is that Pip's insanity results from his coming to understand his own insignificance, both as a black man in white America and as one tiny human in the vast ocean. Ahab, on the other hand, feels himself to have been singled out by, rather than lost in, the vastness of the universe. Pip and Ahab thus represent two opposite psychological extremes.

The conflict between Starbuck and Ahab intensifies in these chapters as Starbuck questions the captain in front of the crew. The two men view the world in different ways, and their differences bring them into collision. Starbuck thinks about home with tenderness, considers the crew, and reasons rather than emotes. His indecision over whether to kill the sleeping Ahab and his thinking aloud recall the scene in *Hamlet* in which Hamlet vacillates about whether to kill Claudius, his father's murderer, while Claudius is praying.

CHAPTERS 126–132

CHAPTER 126: THE LIFE-BUOY

As the *Pequod* approaches the equatorial fishing ground, the sailors think that they hear mermaids or ghosts wailing. The Manxman says that these are the voices of the newly drowned men in the sea. Ahab laughs at this nonsense, telling the men that they have passed a seal colony in the night. Many of the men are superstitious about seals, though, and Ahab's explanation helps little. The next morning, one of the *Pequod*'s crew falls from a masthead. The life buoy that is thrown in after him is old and dried out, and it fills with water and sinks. The man drowns. Starbuck, Stubb, and Flask decide to replace the life buoy with Queequeg's coffin.

CHAPTER 127: THE DECK

This chapter is written in the form of a theatrical dialogue followed by a long soliloquy from Ahab. The carpenter grumbles about having to transform the coffin into a buoy. Ahab, aware of the irony of the substitution, calls the carpenter "unprincipled as the gods" for going through with it. He calls Pip to him to discuss the "wondrous philosophies" of the situation: since Pip's experience in the ocean, the two have been close companions.

CHAPTER 128: THE PEQUOD MEETS THE RACHEL

The *Pequod,* still looking for Moby Dick, encounters the *Rachel.* Captain Gardiner of the *Rachel,* after affirming that he has indeed seen Moby Dick, climbs aboard Ahab's ship and begs Ahab to help him find his son, whose whale boat was lost in the chase after the White Whale. Ahab refuses, not wanting to waste time that could be used in pursuit of Moby Dick.

CHAPTER 129: THE CABIN

Now that Ahab knows that Moby Dick is near, he spends much of his time walking the decks. One night, Pip tries to follow him, telling Ahab that he won't abandon him. Ahab tells Pip to stay in the captain's cabin, lest Pip's insanity cause Ahab's compassion for the boy to distract him from his lust for revenge.

CHAPTER 130: THE HAT

Ahab, shadowed everywhere by Fedallah, remains on deck, ever watchful. The crew falls into a routine of stifled silence. This continuous watch sharpens Ahab's obsession, and he decides that he must be the first to sight the whale. He asks Starbuck to help him get up the main-mast and watch his rope. While Ahab is up there, a black hawk steals his hat, which Ishmael considers a bad omen.

CHAPTER 131: THE PEQUOD MEETS THE DELIGHT

The *Pequod* then runs into the miserably misnamed *Delight*, which has previously encountered Moby Dick, with the unpleasant result of a gutted whale boat and dead men. As the *Pequod* goes by, the *Delight* drops a corpse in the water. The *Delight*'s crew remarks upon the coffin life buoy at the *Pequod*'s stern: to them, it is clear that the coffin is a symbol of doom.

CHAPTER 132: THE SYMPHONY

Ahab and Starbuck exchange stories about their wives and children, and Ahab talks sadly about his wearying quest for Moby Dick. He calls himself a fool and thinks himself pathetic. Starbuck suggests that he give up the chase, but Ahab doubts that he can stop, feeling impelled by fate. As Ahab debates this profound dilemma, Starbuck steals away in despair. When Ahab goes to the other side of the deck to gaze into the water, Fedallah, too, looks over the rail.

ANALYSIS: CHAPTERS 126–132

This set of chapters prepares the reader and the *Pequod*'s crew for the final confrontation with Moby Dick. The atmosphere of doom and the feelings of inevitability grow stronger as the narrative progresses. The sailors, and probably the reader as well, are confused as to which events represent the fulfillment of prophecies of catastrophe and which are in themselves prophecies of disasters to come. The operation of fate and causality is thus unclear, and the justification for Ahab's quest comes to seem strained, as it becomes increasingly apparent, especially in the episodes with the *Rachel* and the *Delight,* that an encounter with Moby Dick is both fated and sure to be fatal. Given that the conclusion seems inevitable, events and objects such as the *Pequod*'s "baptism" as it is splashed by the corpse thrown from the *Delight,* or the coffin attached to the *Pequod*'s stern, take on significance as symbols rather than as causes.

Much has changed aboard the *Pequod* since the beginning of its voyage; most notable is that its power structure has been subverted. Pip, formerly a minor character, is now sitting "in the ship's full middle." Ahab, in fact, tells Pip to sit in his chair as if Pip "were the captain." Pip finds it strange that "a black boy [should play] host to white men with gold lace upon their coats!" He knows that people like him—the young, the black—typically serve older white men like Ahab. It is not clear whether Ahab is in complete control anymore. He asks himself:

> What is it, what nameless, inscrutable, unearthly thing is it; what cozening, hidden lord and master, and cruel, remorseless emperor commands me; that against all natural lovings and longings, I so keep pushing, and crowding, and jamming myself on all the time; recklessly making me ready to do what in my own proper, natural heart, I durst not so much as dare? Is Ahab, Ahab?

In this self-conscious moment, a rare instance of questioning his obsession, Ahab wonders about his free will and his identity. He understands both the folly of his quest and the fact that he is compelled to pursue it by some force that he cannot overcome.

CHAPTER 133–EPILOGUE

CHAPTER 133: THE CHASE—FIRST DAY

Ahab can sense by the smell of a whale in the air that Moby Dick is near. Climbing up to the main royal-mast, Ahab spots Moby Dick and earns himself the doubloon. All of the boats set off in chase of the whale. When Moby Dick finally surfaces, he does so directly beneath Ahab's boat, destroying it and casting its crew into the water. The whale threatens the men, but the *Pequod,* with Starbuck at the helm, drives it away, and the men are rescued by the other boats. The whale then moves away from the ship at a rapid rate, and the boats return to the ship. The men keep watch for Moby Dick, despite the misgivings of Starbuck and others.

CHAPTER 134: THE CHASE—SECOND DAY

Ishmael notes that it is not unprecedented for whalers to give extended pursuit to a particular whale. Ahab, despite the previous day's loss of the boat, is intent on the chase. They do sight Moby Dick again, and the crewmen, in awe of Ahab's wild power and caught up in the thrill, lower three boats. Starbuck again remains on board the *Pequod*. Ahab tries to attack Moby Dick head on this time, but again the whale is triumphant. Despite the harpoons in his side, he destroys the boats carrying Flask and Stubb by dashing them against one another. He also nearly kills Ahab's crew with the tangle of harpoons and lances caught in the line coming from his side. Ahab manages to cut and then reattach the line, removing the cluster of weapons.

Moby Dick then capsizes Ahab's boat. Ahab's whale-bone leg is snapped off in the mishap, and Ahab curses his body's weakness. Upon returning to the Pequod, Ahab finds out that Fedallah has drowned, dragged down by Ahab's own line, fulfilling one element of Fedallah's prophecy concerning Ahab's death—that Ahab would die after Fedallah. Starbuck begs Ahab to desist, but Ahab, convinced that he is only the "Fates' lieutenant," responds that he must continue to pursue the whale. The carpenter hastily makes Ahab a new leg from the remnants of his harpoon boat.

CHAPTER 135: THE CHASE—THIRD DAY

Towards thee I roll, thou all-destroying but
unconquering whale; to the last I grapple with thee;
from hell's heart I stab at thee.
                                            (See QUOTATIONS, *p. 77)*

The crew seeks the White Whale for a third time but sees nothing until Ahab realizes, "Aye, he's chasing me now; not I, him—that's bad." They turn the ship around completely, and Ahab mounts the masthead himself. He sights the spout and comes back down to the deck again. As he gets into his boat and leaves Starbuck in charge, the two men exchange a poignant moment in which Ahab asks to shake hands with his first mate and the first mate tries to tell him not to go. Sharks bite at the oars as the boats pull away. Starbuck laments Ahab's certain doom. Ahab sees Moby Dick breach. The whale damages the other two boats, but Ahab's remains intact. Ahab sees Fedallah's corpse strapped to the whale by turns of rope and realizes that he is seeing the first hearse that Fedallah had predicted, in the sense that a hearse is a vehicle—here, the whale—that carries a corpse.

The whale goes down again, and Ahab rows close to the ship. He tells Tashtego to find another flag and nail it to the main masthead, as the Pequod's flag has somehow been removed from its usual spot. The boats sight the Moby Dick again and go after him. Moby Dick turns around and heads for the Pequod at full speed. He smashes the ship, which goes down without its captain. The ship, Ahab realizes, is the second hearse of Fedallah's prophecy, since it entombs its crew in "American" wood. Impassioned, Ahab is now determined to strike at Moby Dick with all of his power. After darting the whale, Ahab is caught around the neck by the flying line and dragged under the sea—the final element of Fedallah's prophesy. Tashtego, meanwhile, still tries to nail the flag to the ship's spar as it goes down. He catches a sky-hawk in mid-hammer, and the screaming bird, folded in the flag, goes down with everything else. The vortex from the sinking Pequod pulls the remaining harpoon boats and crew down with it.

Epilogue

Ishmael is the only survivor of the Pequod's encounter with Moby Dick. He escapes only because he had been thrown clear of the area in the wreck of Ahab's harpoon boat. Queequeg's coffin bobs up and becomes Ishmael's life buoy. A day after the wreck, the Rachel saves Ishmael as she continues to search for her own lost crew.

Analysis: Chapter 133–Epilogue

Ahab's long-awaited encounter with Moby Dick brings to mind the drawn-out, fantastic battle scenes of myth and epic. He has sought the whale for a full year, the traditional time span of an epic quest. He now battles the whale for three days, stopping each night to rearm himself and repair the day's damage. However, Ahab is fated to lose, and he knows it. The whale seems to toy with the audacious humans, as it surfaces directly beneath their boats and sends a cluster of tangled harpoons and lances whizzing dangerously close to the sailors. Like an annoyed god, the whale means to teach these humans a lesson; Ahab will be punished for his arrogance. By the morning of the third day, Ahab has come to an understanding of the forces that drive him. "Ahab never thinks," he says aloud, "he only feels, feels, feels; . . . to think's audacity. God only has that right and privilege." By framing his quest as an emotional rather than an intellectual one, Ahab admits his own irrationality. Revenge, justice, and other such lofty ideals can be sought only by divine powers; man is too limited in his knowledge and his clout to do much more than react to the world around him.

A fatalist to the last, Ahab doesn't flee the whale, although anyone with common sense surely would have sailed the *Pequod* out of the whale's range at top speed after the first day's defeats. Ahab's death should not be read as a suicide, though. To the obsessed captain, each encounter with the whale fulfills a part of the prophecies made concerning his ultimate end. By going forward with the fight, he completes a larger design and gives his life and death a greater significance than it would have had otherwise. Only figures of importance—heroes, gods, martyrs—have their deaths foretold. By committing himself to a struggle he cannot win, Ahab becomes the stuff of legend.

Ahab's death suggests itself as a metaphor for the human condition. Man, of limited knowledge and meager powers, lives and dies struggling against forces that he can neither understand nor conquer. By continuing to fight the whale even when defeat is imminent, Ahab acts out, in dramatic form, the fate of all men. His request that Tashtego nail a new flag to the mast of the sinking ship is a sign not of defiance but of recognition that to be mortal is to persevere in the face of certain defeat, and that such perseverance is the highest and most heroic accomplishment of man.

Ishmael survives by floating on Queequeg's coffin, which had been transformed into the *Pequod*'s life buoy. The coffin symbolizes not only resurrection but also the persistence of narratives. Queequeg has cheated death by inscribing his tattoos on the coffin. Ahab too has cheated death, in a sense, since he will continue to live on through Ishmael's narration. The conclusion of *Moby-Dick* is laced with such ironies, which are the matter of myth, for *Moby-Dick*, though it encompasses allegory, adventure, and many other genres, is more than anything a myth about the follies of man.

IMPORTANT QUOTATIONS EXPLAINED

1. How it is I know not; but there is no place like a bed for
    confidential disclosures between friends. Man and wife,
    they say, there open the very bottom of their souls to each
    other; and some old couples often lie and chat over old times
    till nearly morning. Thus, then, in our hearts' honeymoon,
    lay I and Queequeg—a cosy, loving pair.

This passage comes at the end of Chapter 10, when Ishmael is forced
to share a bed with the tattooed "savage" Queequeg at the Spouter-
Inn. At first horrified, Ishmael is quickly impressed by Queequeg's
dignity and kindness. The homoerotic overtones of their sharing a
bed and staying up much of the night smoking and talking suggests
a profound, close bond born of mutual dependence and a world in
which merit, rather than race or wealth, determines a man's status.
The men aboard the *Pequod* are everything to one another, and the
relationships between them are stronger and more meaningful than
even that between man and wife. Ishmael's willingness to describe
his relationship with Queequeg in such conjugal terms ("honey-
moon") symbolizes his openness to new experiences and people.

2.   Come, Ahab's compliments to ye; come and see if ye can
      swerve me. Swerve me? ye cannot swerve me, else ye swerve
      yourselves! man has ye there. Swerve me? The path to my
      fixed purpose is laid with iron rails, whereon my soul is
      grooved to run. Over unsounded gorges, through the rifled
      hearts of mountains, under torrents' beds, unerringly I rush!
      Naught's an obstacle, naught's an angle to the iron way!

Ahab speaks these words in his soliloquy in Chapter 37, daring anyone to try to divert him from his purpose. Though he is defiant, he is
also accepting of his fate, asserting that he has no control over his
own behavior—he must run along the "iron rails" that have been
laid for him. The powerful rhetoric and strong imagery of this passage are characteristic of Ahab's speech. He uses his skill with language to persuade his crew to take part in his quest for vengeance,
stirring them with suggestions of adventure ("unsounded gorges,"
"rifled hearts of mountains") and inspiring confidence through his
apparent faith in himself as "unerring." Just as Ishmael occasionally
gets lost in digressions, Ahab occasionally gets lost in language,
repeating the phrase "swerve me" until it becomes almost meaning-
less, merely a sound. His speeches thus become a kind of poetry or
music, stirring the listener with their form as much as their content.

QUOTATIONS

3. All that most maddens and torments; all that stirs up the lees of things; all truth with malice in it; all that cracks the sinews and cakes the brain; all the subtle demonisms of life and thought; all evil, to crazy Ahab, were visibly personified, and made practically assailable in Moby Dick. He piled upon the whale's white hump the sum of all the general rage and hate felt by his whole race from Adam down; and then, as if his chest had been a mortar, he burst his hot heart's shell upon it.

This quote, from Chapter 41, is the existential heart of the book; appropriately, the chapter from which it comes shares its title with the White Whale and the novel itself. While many sailors aboard the *Pequod* use legends about particularly large and malevolent whales as a way to manage the fear and danger inherent in whaling, they do not take these legends literally. Ahab, on the other hand, believes that Moby Dick is evil incarnate, and pits himself and humanity in an epic, timeless struggle against the White Whale. His belief that killing Moby Dick will eradicate evil evidences his inability to understand things symbolically: he is too literal a reader of the world around him. Instead of interpreting the loss of his leg as a common consequence of his occupation and perhaps as a punishment for taking excessive risks, he sees it as evidence of evil cosmic forces persecuting him.

QUOTATIONS

4.   There is a wisdom that is woe; but there is a woe that is
       madness. And there is a Catskill eagle in some souls that can
       alike dive down into the blackest gorges, and soar out of
       them again and become invisible in the sunny spaces. And
       even if he for ever flies within the gorge, that gorge is in the
       mountains; so that even in his lowest swoop the mountain
       eagle is still higher than other birds upon the plain, even
       though they soar.

This passage comes at the end of Chapter 96, as Ishmael snaps out
of a hypnotic state brought on by staring into the fires of the try-
works. The image that Ishmael conjures here is typical of his philosophical speculation and his habit of quickly turning from a very literal subject to its metaphorical implications. This passage is a
warning against giving in to escapism—fantasy, daydreaming, suicide—and suggests that woe and madness can be profitable states
for one with enough greatness of soul. For one who is intelligent and
perceptive—whose soul is "in the mountains" and greater than the
average person's—such states of mind provide a higher plane of
existence than contentedness and sanity do for a normal person. In
other words, Ahab may be insane and "for ever . . . within the
gorge," but his inherent greatness makes even his destruction more
important than the mere existence—the "soar[ing]"—of other,
more banal individuals.

5. Towards thee I roll, thou all-destroying but unconquering whale; to the last I grapple with thee; from hell's heart I stab at thee; for hate's sake I spit my last breath at thee. Sink all coffins and all hearses to one common pool! and since neither can be mine, let me then tow to pieces, while still chasing thee, though tied to thee, thou damned whale! Thus, I give up the spear!

Ahab utters these words—his last—after Moby Dick destroys the *Pequod,* in Chapter 135. As the action picks up pace, the sense of tragedy becomes heightened. These words, Shakespearean in tone, are meant to match the dramatic nature of the situation in which they are spoken. Ahab dies as he began, defiant but aware of his fate. The whale is "all-destroying but unconquering": its victory has been inevitable, but it has not defeated Ahab's spirit. In an ultimate demonstration of defiance, Ahab uses his "last breath" to curse the whale and fate. He is, spiritually, already in "hell's heart," and he acquiesces to his own imminent death. This final climactic explosion of eloquence and theatricality is followed by an overwhelming silence, as the whale disappears and everything and everyone but Ishmael is pulled below the ocean's surface.

QUOTATIONS

Key Facts

FULL TITLE
Moby-Dick; or *The Whale*

AUTHOR
Herman Melville

TYPE OF WORK
Novel

GENRE
Epic, adventure story, quest tale, allegory, tragedy

LANGUAGE
English

TIME AND PLACE WRITTEN
Between 1850 and 1851, in Pittsfield, Massachusetts, and New York City

DATE OF FIRST PUBLICATION
1851

PUBLISHER
Harper & Brothers in America (simultaneously published in England by Richard Bentley as THE WHALE)

NARRATOR
Ishmael, a junior member of the *Pequod*'s crew, casts himself as the author, recounting the events of the voyage after he has acquired more experience and studied the whale extensively.

POINT OF VIEW
Ishmael narrates in a combination of first and third person, describing events as he saw them and providing his own thoughts. He presents the thoughts and feelings of the other characters only as an outside observer might infer them.

TONE
Ironic, celebratory, philosophical, dramatic, hyperbolic

TENSE
Past

SETTING (TIME)

1830s or 1840s

SETTING (PLACE)

Aboard the whaling ship the *Pequod,* in the Pacific, Atlantic, and Indian Oceans

MAJOR CONFLICT

Ahab dedicates his ship and crew to destroying Moby Dick, a white sperm whale, because he sees this whale as the living embodiment of all that is evil and malignant in the universe. By ignoring the physical dangers that this quest entails, setting himself against other men, and presuming to understand and fight evil on a cosmic scale, Ahab arrogantly defies the limitations imposed upon human beings.

RISING ACTION

Ahab announces his quest to the other sailors and nails the doubloon to the mast; the *Pequod* encounters various ships with news and stories about Moby Dick

CLIMAX

In Chapter 132, "The Symphony," Ahab interrogates himself and his quest in front of Starbuck, and realizes that he does not have the will to turn aside from his purpose.

FALLING ACTION

The death of Ahab and the destruction of the *Pequod* by Moby Dick; Ishmael, the only survivor of the *Pequod*'s sinking, floats on a coffin and is rescued by another whaling ship, the *Rachel.*

THEMES

The limits of knowledge; the deceptiveness of fate; the exploitative nature of whaling

MOTIFS

Whiteness; surfaces and depths

SYMBOLS

The *Pequod* symbolizes doom; Moby Dick, on an objective level, symbolizes humankind's inability to understand the world; Queequeg's coffin symbolizes both life and death

KEY FACTS

FORESHADOWING

Foreshadowing in *Moby-Dick* is extensive and inescapable: everything from the Pequod's ornamentation to the behavior of schools of fish to the appearance of a giant squid is read as an omen of the eventual catastrophic encounter with Moby Dick.

KEY FACTS

STUDY QUESTIONS & ESSAY TOPICS

STUDY QUESTIONS

1. MOBY-DICK *features several characters who seem insane. How does insanity relate to this story? How do these characters contrast with one another?*

Ishmael describes Ahab as mad in his narration, and it does indeed seem mad to try to fight the forces of nature or God. However, some of the other characters in the novel whom Ishmael labels insane— notably Pip and Gabriel—might be viewed as wise rather than crazy, thus calling into question the possibility of making a clear distinction between sanity and insanity. Gabriel, the prophet figure aboard the *Jeroboam,* behaves irrationally and makes a number of ridiculous-sounding predictions. If viewed in a certain light, however, his prophecies sound not like silly attempts to foresee the future but like cleverly phrased efforts to effect change aboard his ship. Gabriel's prophecies are aimed at gaining the crew just treatment from the ship's officers and at avoiding the danger that will come from trying to hunt Moby Dick. Like Ahab, he manipulates the crew's superstitions and religious beliefs in order to gather support. But whereas Ahab's obsession is monomaniacal and selfish, Gabriel's "madness" is a response to irrational and unjust behavior on the part of those who control his ship.

2. *Ishmael frequently refers to the relationships between men in terms normally used to describe heterosexual romantic relationships. What is the literal and symbolic importance of homoeroticism in MOBY-DICK?*

Ishmael and Queequeg are depicted in bed together several times and are frequently described as "married" or "wedded" to each other. When they wake in the Spouter-Inn, Queequeg has his arms around Ishmael in a seemingly conjugal embrace. Melville uses the vocabulary of love and marriage to suggest the strength and closeness of the bonds between men at sea. Marriage is one of the institutions upon which society on land is organized, but there are no women aboard the *Pequod*. Instead, the crew develops a bond based on mutual dependence: they need each other to stay alive and are thus literally "wedded" to one another. In the absence of other relationships, they become everything to one another—metaphorical parents, siblings, best friends, and lovers. The replacement of heterosexual relationships, so central to conventional society, with homoerotic ones also signals a rejection of other aspects of life on land, such as racism, economic stratification, and limited opportunities for social mobility. Queequeg, for example, is taken aboard the *Pequod* for his expert marksmanship, despite his nonwhite skin.

3. *Describe the playlike scenes interspersed throughout* MOBY-DICK. *What is the function of these scenes? In what ways do they differ from the rest of the narrative?*

These scenes fall into two major categories: dramatic dialogues among several characters and soliloquies from a single character, often Ahab. The latter capture moments that Ishmael, the narrator, could not possibly have witnessed. Ahab must maintain his composure and certainty in front of his crew; it is only in private that he can express doubt or regret. These scenes are used to build dramatic tension, as they would in a play: Ahab senses the approach of catastrophe, which his soliloquies communicate to the reader by voicing his feeling of doom. The dialogue scenes frequently alternate with chapters that contain digressions from the plot. (Ishmael's measurements of the whale's skeleton, for example.) In this context, they become very suspenseful, as the plot is advanced purely through the authentic-seeming speech interactions of the sailors. Finally, by hearkening back to well-known dramatic works, these dramatic scenes also remind the reader of *Moby-Dick*'s thematic connections to tragic drama, particularly Shakespeare.

Suggested Essay Topics

1. *Why does Ishmael include so many digressions in his narrative? Why does he draw on so many other disciplines (geology, art, biology)? Choose one of these digressions (the chapter on "Cetology," for example) and discuss the ways in which it comments on the main narrative.*

2. *Describe Ishmael's method of narration. Is he reliable or unreliable as a narrator? Why is he the one to tell this story? What would the narrative have been like if Ahab were the narrator?*

3. *How is the concept of fate used to organize the narrative? Does fate justify Ahab's actions? What is the relationship between fate and prophecy? What does fate have to do with religion, particularly Christianity?*

4. *Explain some of the biblical references in* MOBY-DICK. *How does Melville use the Bible as a literary model and as a source for thematic material?*

REVIEW & RESOURCES

QUIZ

1. Where does Ishmael want to go to find a berth on a whaling ship?

   A. Boston
   B. Nantucket
   C. New Bedford
   D. New York

2. Which biblical figure is the focus of Father Mapple's sermon?

   A. Job
   B. Solomon
   C. Isaiah
   D. Jonah

3. Which body part has Ahab lost to Moby Dick?

   A. His leg
   B. His arm
   C. His eye
   D. His fingers

4. What is the name of Ahab's ship?

   A. The *Town-Ho*
   B. The *Rachel*
   C. The *Samuel Enderby*
   D. The *Pequod*

5. After what is Ahab's ship named?

   A. Its owner
   B. A vanished tribe of Native Americans
   C. A species of whale
   D. A biblical character

6. For what were whales primarily hunted?

   A. Oil
   B. Skin
   C. Meat
   D. Fins

7. Which of the following characters falls overboard and goes insane as a result?

   A. Tashtego
   B. Pip
   C. Queequeg
   D. Starbuck

8. Who rescues Tashtego when he falls overboard inside the whale's head?

   A. Ishmael
   B. Stubb
   C. Fedallah
   D. Queequeg

9. What does Ahab nail to the ship's mast to motivate his crew in his quest for Moby Dick?

   A. A gold coin
   B. A severed head
   C. A drawing of Moby Dick
   D. A pirate flag

10. Which of the following characters survives the Pequod's sinking?

    A. Pip
    B. Ahab
    C. Flask
    D. None of the above

REVIEW & RESOURCES

11. What keeps Ishmael afloat after the Pequod sinks?

     A.   A coffin
     B.   A barrel of oil
     C.   A lifeboat
     D.   A mattress

12. What does the crew look for to indicate the presence of a whale?

     A.   Fins
     B.   Spouts
     C.   Seabirds
     D.   Lightning

13. What frightens Ishmael the most about Moby Dick?

     A.   The whale's size
     B.   The whale's teeth
     C.   The whiteness of the whale
     D.   The sounds that the whale makes

14. What is cetology?

     A.   The skill of navigation
     B.   The study of old manuscripts
     C.   The process used to render oil out of a whale
     D.   The study of whales

15. What covers Queequeg's skin?

     A.   Scars
     B.   Tattoos
     C.   Hair
     D.   Blisters

16. What does Ishmael have tattooed on his forearm?

     A.   A naked woman
     B.   A spouting whale
     C.   The dimensions of a whale
     D.   A passage from the Book of Job

17. With what is the Pequod adorned?

    A. Sperm whale teeth
    B. American flags
    C. Red paint
    D. Whale fins

18. From what is Ahab's false leg made?

    A. A whale's jawbone
    B. Wood
    C. An elephant's tusk
    D. Leather

19. With which of the following characters does Ishmael share a bed at the Spouter-Inn?

    A. Starbuck
    B. Fedallah
    C. Bildad
    D. Queequeg

20. Out of what is Fedallah's turban made?

    A. Whale skin
    B. His hair
    C. Silk from China
    D. Dried seaweed

21. How does the Pequod sink?

    A. She is rammed by Moby Dick.
    B. She is overloaded with oil.
    C. She gets lost in a storm.
    D. She is rammed by another ship.

22. Who owns the Pequod?

    A. Father Mapple
    B. Captain Ahab
    C. The town of Nantucket
    D. Bildad and Peleg

REVIEW & RESOURCES

23. With what does Queequeg sleep?

    A.   The statue of his god
    B.   His harpoon
    C.   A cat
    D.   A bottle of rum

24. Ahab's mates include

    A.   Starbuck
    B.   Stubb
    C.   Flask
    D.   All of the above

25. What does Ahab see when he studies the gold doubloon nailed to the mast?

    A.   Moby Dick
    B.   Himself
    C.   God
    D.   The face of Evil

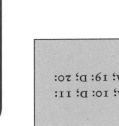

REVIEW & RESOURCES

ANSWER KEY:
1: B; 2: D; 3: A; 4: D; 5: B; 6: A; 7: B; 8: D; 9: A; 10: D; 11: A; 12: B; 13: C; 14: D; 15: B; 16: C; 17: A; 18: A; 19: D; 20: B; 21: A; 22: D; 23: B; 24: D; 25: B

Suggestions for Further Reading

BENDER, BERT. *Sea Brothers: The Tradition of American Sea Fiction from* Moby-Dick *to the Present.* Philadelphia: University of Pennsylvania Press, 1998.

BLOOM, HAROLD, ed. *Herman Melville's* Moby-Dick. New York: Chelsea House, 1996.

CAMERON, SHARON. *The Corporeal Self: Allegories of the Body in Melville and Hawthorne.* Baltimore: Johns Hopkins University Press, 1989.

COWAN, BAINARD. *Exiled Waters:* Moby-Dick *and the Crisis of Allegory.* Baton Rouge: Louisiana State University Press, 1982.

HEIMERT, ALAN. Moby-Dick *and American Political Symbolism.* Cambridge, Massachusetts: The Eliot House Edition, 1991.

LEVINE, ROBERT S., ed. *The Cambridge Companion to Herman Melville.* Cambridge, UK: Cambridge University Press, 1998.

MORRISON, TONI. "Unspeakable Things Unspoken: The Afro-American Presence in American Literature." In *Within the Circle: An Anthology of African American Literary Criticism from the Harlem Renaissance to the Present,* ed. Angelyn Mitchell. Durham, North Carolina: Duke University Press, 1994.

OLSON, CHARLES. *Call Me Ishmael.* Baltimore: Johns Hopkins University Press, 1997.

POST-LAURIA, SHEILA. *Correspondent Colorings: Melville in the Marketplace.* Amherst: University of Massachusetts Press, 1996.

SLADE, LEONARD A. *Symbolism in Herman Melville's* Moby-Dick: *From the Satanic to the Divine.* Lewiston, New York: E. Mellen Press, 1998.

REVIEW & RESOURCES

SparkNotes™ Literature Guides

1984
The Adventures of Huckleberry Finn
The Adventures of Tom Sawyer
The Aeneid
All Quiet on the Western Front
And Then There Were None
Angela's Ashes
Animal Farm
Anna Karenina
Anne of Green Gables
Anthem
Antony and Cleopatra
Aristotle's Ethics
As I Lay Dying
As You Like It
Atlas Shrugged
The Awakening
The Autobiography of Malcolm X
The Bean Trees
The Bell Jar
Beloved
Beowulf
Billy Budd
Black Boy
Bless Me, Ultima
The Bluest Eye
Brave New World
The Brothers Karamazov
The Call of the Wild
Candide
The Canterbury Tales
Catch-22
The Catcher in the Rye
The Chocolate War
The Chosen
Cold Mountain
Cold Sassy Tree
The Color Purple
The Count of Monte Cristo
Crime and Punishment
The Crucible
Cry, the Beloved Country
Cyrano de Bergerac
David Copperfield

Death of a Salesman
The Death of Socrates
The Diary of a Young Girl
A Doll's House
Don Quixote
Dr. Faustus
Dr. Jekyll and Mr. Hyde
Dracula
Dune
East of Eden
Edith Hamilton's Mythology
Emma
Ethan Frome
Fahrenheit 451
Fallen Angels
A Farewell to Arms
Farewell to Manzanar
Flowers for Algernon
For Whom the Bell Tolls
The Fountainhead
Frankenstein
The Giver
The Glass Menagerie
Gone With the Wind
The Good Earth
The Grapes of Wrath
Great Expectations
The Great Gatsby
Greek Classics
Grendel
Gulliver's Travels
Hamlet
The Handmaid's Tale
Hard Times
Harry Potter and the Sorcerer's Stone
Heart of Darkness
Henry IV, Part I
Henry V
Hiroshima
The Hobbit
The House of Seven Gables
I Know Why the Caged Bird Sings
The Iliad
Inferno
Inherit the Wind
Invisible Man

Jane Eyre
Johnny Tremain
The Joy Luck Club
Julius Caesar
The Jungle
The Killer Angels
King Lear
The Last of the Mohicans
Les Miserables
A Lesson Before Dying
The Little Prince
Little Women
Lord of the Flies
The Lord of the Rings
Macbeth
Madame Bovary
A Man for All Seasons
The Mayor of Casterbridge
The Merchant of Venice
A Midsummer Night's Dream
Moby Dick
Much Ado About Nothing
My Antonia
Narrative of the Life of Frederick Douglass
Native Son
The New Testament
Night
Notes from Underground
The Odyssey
The Oedipus Plays
Of Mice and Men
The Old Man and the Sea
The Old Testament
Oliver Twist
The Once and Future King
One Day in the Life of Ivan Denisovich
One Flew Over the Cuckoo's Nest
One Hundred Years of Solitude
Othello
Our Town
The Outsiders

Paradise Lost
A Passage to India
The Pearl
The Picture of Dorian Gray
Poe's Short Stories
A Portrait of the Artist as a Young Man
Pride and Prejudice
The Prince
A Raisin in the Sun
The Red Badge of Courage
The Republic
Richard III
Robinson Crusoe
Romeo and Juliet
The Scarlet Letter
A Separate Peace
Silas Marner
Sir Gawain and the Green Knight
Slaughterhouse-Five
Snow Falling on Cedars
Song of Solomon
The Sound and the Fury
Steppenwolf
The Stranger
Streetcar Named Desire
The Sun Also Rises
A Tale of Two Cities
The Taming of the Shrew
The Tempest
Tess of the d'Ubervilles
Their Eyes Were Watching God
Things Fall Apart
The Things They Carried
To Kill a Mockingbird
To the Lighthouse
Treasure Island
Twelfth Night
Ulysses
Uncle Tom's Cabin
Walden
War and Peace
Wuthering Heights
A Yellow Raft in Blue Water